To Harvey,

So lovely to met
that you for your support

2018

Black Girl White Skin

A LIFE IN STORIES

NATALIE DEVORA

TABLE OF CONTENTS

When we speak we are afraid our words will not be heard or welcomed. But when we are silent, we are still afraid. So it is better to speak.
AUDRE LORDE

PROLOGUE

When I was four years old, I begged to be taught to read. Even then I recognized the value of words. Books allowed me entry into the lives of others. The challenges with my vision meant reading required my eyes to be mere inches from the page, but that did not deter me. By ten I'd read every book in my school library. Books were the consolation prize for not being able to play outdoors. Having albinism meant my skin bore no natural protection against the sun's harsh rays. Consequently, I was kept indoors to avoid sunburns.

At twelve I was granted permission to take the city bus to the main branch of the Oakland Public Library. I devoured Maya Angelou's I Know Why the Caged Bird Sings and Toni Morrison's The Bluest Eye in a quest to find myself, to discover stories that mirrored my young life. While each possessed elements of my world, neither reflected my personal reality. In my twenties I discovered the works of Audre Lorde and Michelle

Cliff. Once again, their words spoke to aspects of my identity, but not fully. I realized I would have to tell my story.

When I embarked on this project, I believed I would chronicle the first part of my life, one that focused on albinism. However, as I immersed myself in memory, spoke with family elders, close friends, and my writing community, it became clear there were many stories to share. I delved deeply into the recesses of my psyche. I unearthed experiences I'd locked away, examining their nuances. I confronted each one head-on. I discovered the massive work healing requires. I took baths. Lots of baths.

I called upon my ancestors, specifically my two grandmothers, Laura Devoria Eastman Lester and Jewel King Young. They were powerful storytellers. I sought their strength to hold me, push me, demand I give my all to the various aspects of my history, which has enabled me to become who I am today.

At one point I became stuck, the recalling was excruciating. The key players, now all deceased, attempted to silence me. Their voices whispered, whined, even threatened me against claiming my truth. My daughter presented me with a T-shirt, emblazoned with the following words: I am my ancestors' wildest dreams. This was exactly what I needed to propel me forward. Once again, they were guiding me, enveloping me in safety, fueling me through the sludge of silence.

A part of me is compelled to warn you that this book, these stories, may trigger you. And yet I'm also inclined to not, so that the reader may form her own opinion. The former is the me that wishes to take care of people, to prepare them for what lies ahead. While the latter may be the wiser, allowing for points of celebration, anger, sorrow, and more.

A friend affectionately calls me Cura, short for Curandera, healer. My remedies include language, courage, tears, silence, laughter, joy. My work is through stories.

ONE CHILD

The idea for this story came to me as I recalled my daughter's birth. Her arrival had been a joyous event. After years of trying to conceive, this miracle, though yet unborn, baby entered our lives. As I wrote Jewel's story a few years ago, the story of my own birth emerged, murky yet insistent. I began to question family members, to shake their memories free. Initially I received polite chatter about how happy everyone was when I made my grand debut. Then slowly, after further probing, cousins and aunts divulged more, like pebbles long buried under the soft mud at the bottom of a lake. These were the unearthed truths of course—the facts, the surprise, the shock, and the horror of what my arrival confirmed. For I was a secret made manifest. I was the physical embodiment of my mother having been molested by her father.

What follows is my personal view on my birth and the impact this had not only on my mother and my grandparents, yet ultimately on me.

I was cocooned from the harshness of outside comments, judgments, and stares until I went to elementary school. During my first years, I played with my older brother and younger sister, and we were all differently colored. Difference was no matter for my concern. Protected from the harsh realities of the world, my early years were happy ones. Like all children, I learned to crawl, climb, and walk in that order, terrifying my poor mother. She would make weekly visits to the doctor with me, which she hated. Not me, but the visits. It was 1962, and you just didn't see Black women with white-skinned babies they claimed were theirs. People were nosy, often asking who I belonged to. When I was tiny, she'd cover my head with a blanket to avoid unwelcome comments. Mama bore the brunt of the assumptions, ignorance, and ridicule of others, both strangers and family. She would learn to block out the strangers or tell them to mind their own business. Family was harder.

The Eastman and Lester families were huge. Word spread quickly about the baby. About me. What the cousins remember is hearing that Anna Mary, as my mother was called then, had had a white baby. The aunts and uncles learned the child wasn't normal and there needed to be a prayer circle as soon as was possible.

The Eastman uncles and aunts arrived at the hospital a couple of days after I was born. They gathered around my mother and me, praying and laying hands on newborn me, seeking forgiveness for angering God. The prayer was supposed to heal me, because, as the story goes, there was no color in my eyes. After an hour of prayer and laying on of hands, it was said that the color returned to my eyes, providing relief to everyone, including the doctors.

It would be these same relatives who would shiver, glad it wasn't them having to deal with the situation. It would be their whispers about the wrongdoings of my grandfather toward his daughter that would have them thanking the Lord and tsk-tsk-ing at the same time. I was told there was some sort of family barbecue at my grandparents' house where there were mostly Lesters in attendance. The Lester women were more accepting.

When I consider today what my birth must have been like and how I would have been received by the family, I tend to believe the story went more like this . . .

On the day I was born, the old blue Rambler sped through the silent city streets. In the predawn, the buildings appeared in shadow. Mother sat, eyes closed, feeling my head pushing down on her cervix. "Hurry up, Daddy. She's not gonna wait long." Moaning in pain, Anna Mary could no longer be silent. She wanted me to be born, out of her body. She wanted to be free of me.

When the old blue Rambler pulled up to the building, my grandfather helped my mother, who was already sweating from the pain of labor, out of the car and into the hospital.

The nurse helped her to a room asking, "First time, dear?"

Mother shook her head.

"Second? Third?"

The contractions were coming so close together.

"Third time," she finally managed.

The nurse, a solidly built woman with brown hair nodded in understanding. She eased Mother onto the table. Mother sighed with relief. She'd made it. I was coming quickly. She was pushed into the delivery room where a doctor and nurses waited. Someone wiped her face with a cool towel. In a matter of minutes, I pushed my way down the canal, leaving the only safety I would ever know. My body slid from between her strong brown thighs. Those thighs which had been forced open by her father. Pushed apart in ownership; the thighs of a teenage girl already a mother at fifteen. In his mind, these thighs were his right. They and she belonged to him.

I entered into a brightly lit, very loud world. I had pushed my way out of my mother's womb less than five minutes after she'd arrived at the hospital.

Nevertheless, on the day I was born, there was a particular silence. A pause, before the fact could be approached. The doctor passed me over to the nurse who weighed and measured me. 8.5 pounds and 19 inches. She took the time to clean my body, all the while inspecting me. Amniotic fluid was washed from me, head to feet. I screamed in rebellion, wanting instead the safety of Mama's womb.

Everyone whispered, marveling at the sight of me. "How did that happen?" one nurse bravely asked. This was what everyone in the room wanted to know but dared not say out loud. The tired doctor shook his head, indicating his uncertainty. My body flailed, curling up at the sensation of cool air. I was checked again and again. Ten fingers, ten toes, strong lungs. Eyes closed, I made my debut.

"Is the father White?"

"Don't think so," came the response. No one knew what to make of me.

My mother had been forgotten, left on the table alone. All she knew was something wasn't quite right. "Bring me my little girl!" she called out. Her heart was beginning to race. For a moment, she wondered if she should be demanding anything of the doctor. She was a Negro girl, and they were White. But the baby . . . something wasn't right. Fear gripped her. She was soothed by a nurse, or at least the nurse attempted to soothe her. Mother would have none of it. She waited. She waited to meet me.

On the day I was born, no one expected me to be White. Well, not White, but albino. The doctors and nurses regarded me in silence. I was unexpected. For, at first, I was a thing to be gawked at. The doctor had heard of albinism, of course, though he had never delivered one.

I was taken away, weighed and measured, poked and prodded. My fingers and toes counted yet again, skin checked, mouth cleared. Only after these things were done was I thoroughly cleaned up and made ready to meet Mama.

She'd been asking for me, waiting anxiously. She knew something wasn't quite right. The doctor asked her foolish questions about her husband's race. She answered as calmly as she could, heart still beating fast. Finally, after waiting forever, I was placed in Mama's arms.

Pulling the blanket back she saw my white hair, my pale skin, closed eyes. "Oh," was all she could say. She knew she'd been punished. Punished for the shameful deed. "What . . . how . . . ?" Questions half formed on her lips couldn't make themselves fully known. I was given a name, then rushed away.

Mother was settled into her room, but she wasn't happy. She was scared. Scared that God was punishing her. This was her fault. Her fault she'd become pregnant. Her fault she wasn't able to fight her father off. Her fault this baby didn't look the way she should.

On the day I was born, my grandmother resorted to prayer. Laura D always resorted to prayer. This day, she first prayed that her daughter—my mother—would make it to the hospital in time. Laura had lain awake in bed listening to her daughter pace. She lay waiting for the call, which came around 4 a.m. At that moment, the entire house rose to get my mother to where she needed to be. My brother was scooped from bed, wrapped in a quilt. His nearly three-year-old body heavy with sleep. He was delivered into the waiting arms of my Aunt Louise, grandmother's twin sister who placed Greg into bed with one of her boys.

On the day I was born, grandmother sat in the waiting room, waiting for news. She watched her husband make tracks in the floor walking back and forth. Laura knew better than suggest he sit down. He wouldn't. She watched as he took up space, his presence filling the room. Anna Mary had just made it. They both could hear the sound of the baby's cry. "Thank the Lord," she said to herself aloud. When the clock indicated that another hour had passed, the doctor emerged, not meeting their gaze.

"It's a girl," he told them. "Healthy, but—" He paused. "Well, you should see for yourself." The doctor walked away, his hand rustling through his hair.

"What was he saying, Clint?" Looking up at her husband, Laura didn't understand. What did the doctor's words mean? The couple was taken to their daughter. Her back was to them as they entered the room.

"Girl, what's wrong with you? Look at me," Laura demanded of her daughter. Anna Mary lay unmoving.

A nurse walked in carrying a pink-wrapped bundle. She walked cautiously to the grandparents, pulling back the blanket, revealing soft downy white hair and pale skin. They gasped. Both stood still in utter surprise.

"This can't be," my grandfather said, shaking his head in disbelief. They could hear their daughter's sobs.

Between sobs, Anna Mary managed, "It's so. That's the baby. I named her Natalie. I'm sorry, Mama," was all she could choke out before tears overtook her again.

"She's a healthy girl," the nurse said in the awkward silence. "Eight pounds, six ounces, and nineteen inches long. She looks like an angel."

Laura gingerly took the pink bundle from the nurse. Looking at her first granddaughter, she asked, "Lord, what you gonna do with this one? Lord, forgive us. Lord, protect us." Placing me in Mama's arms, she said, "Now hold her, Anna Mary. You've got to hold her."

I lay next to Mama quietly. After a few minutes, she looked at me, really taking me in. I looked back at her with pale, translucent eyes. My grandparents looked at each other. Neither spoke, yet both knew the aunts and uncles needed to be called.

On the day I was born, I was a miracle. I defied what was expected. I came into the world a White child to all appearances, a White child born to a Negro mother. I was an unknown. The product of incest and rape. I was a reminder. I was the embodiment, the physical proof of what inbreeding creates. My mother, not more than a girl herself, had been used by her father for years. She was his property to do with as he willed. The secret of my origins remained unspoken. No one in the family would dare speak the truth. They were all complicit to the crime. Each knowing, yet no one acting on my mother's behalf. Instead, there were whispers about keeping their own daughters away from my mother's father.

Once, when I was in my twenties, a cousin told me that my grandmother's brothers had gone to her. The brothers let her know there was a solution to her husband's wandering hands. A permanent solution. The three men spoke with impatient voices, each seeing the pain their niece endured. Yet their hands were tied by their sister as she commanded they leave her husband be. She defended him, saying he'd done no wrong. The brothers left, hands balled into fists, faces tight with anger. They honored their sister's wishes.

On the day I was born, a plan was made for me. A plan I would have to step into. My destiny was already charted. Little did I know the impact my birth would make.

Or that my life would be spectacular.

A nurse eventually placed me, cleaned and swaddled, into mother's arms. Her first response to meeting me was "Oh." She stared at me, learning my features. My skin, nearly translucent, reminded her of dolls she'd played with when she was younger.

My eyes were scrunched closed to the light filling the room. She could identify her nose and what would later prove to be her lips. These lips were also the lips of her father. She tried not to think of her father as she held her new daughter. Yet her mind was consumed with guilt, as this baby, too, was his.

The aunts and uncles on the Eastman side gathered in a vigil. They prayed, seeking forgiveness from God. They prayed for me, asking the Lord to heal me. "Lord, please make this child normal." The word had gotten out quickly that my eyes had been nearly clear. In their prayer, the aunts and uncles begged God, "Give this child some color in her eyes, Lord, so that she might see you and be healed."

Four days after my birth, I was brought home. Relatives gathered at my grandparents' home, waiting. They spoke in low voices, giving thanks to God that they had normal children. Those normal children ran about playing in the backyard as Grandfather pulled up in the old blue Rambler, carrying his wife, his daughter, and the new baby. He was a proud man. He knew all the relations would be waiting. That's what everyone did. They gathered to welcome the newest addition to any family. Children were to be celebrated. Today, the celebration would have to wait.

The aunts had worked all day preparing food for everyone. There was fried chicken, potato salad, creamed corn, and collard greens. There was a five-layer cake from Aunt Annie for whom my mother was named. There was pound cake, and there was peach cobbler. He knew these things would be there. And the day had already been long. He was hungry.

As he opened the door helping his daughter from the old car, Clint Lester made up his mind. He had issues with his wife's people, but today he would have things be different. Yes, he told himself, different. He decided he would take pride in what was his. His daughter. His granddaughter. This baby of his was special. She was his china doll.

Opening the front door, CJ greeted the women with a warm bellow. He was welcomed with a series of hellos from the women. Behind him was his daughter carrying the new baby, and behind her came his wife. Laura was hugged by her sisters while they made their niece sit on the sofa. The women fussed about Anna Mary, propping her up with pillows, placing a glass of water in front of her, helping her to settle in with the pink-wrapped bundle.

Finally, Aunt Rose couldn't stand it any longer. "Now let me see her, sweetheart." It was her gentle tone that caused the girl to relax some, yet bracing for the inevitable.

Outside the men sat, knowing they would be last to see the child. They knew this was the women's time. They were charged with, well, not exactly looking after the children, but more like keeping order so their women could tend to Anna Mary. It was also their task to make ice cream. Ice cream made the old-fashioned way, with a wooden barrel and a metal insert in which the cream mixture was churned. Surrounding the metal cylinder, ice and rock salt was packed, creating the right temperature needed for the rich, sweet, ice cream. The men stood around, each encouraging the children to turn the handle until the salt and ice became too difficult for small hands. One by one the men flexed their muscles, moving the crank on the ice cream maker.

William, Mack, and Samuel were Laura's brothers, the ones who had approached my grandmother with a solution that was firmly rejected. Jim was grandfather's only brother. Each man was good looking. Jim had skin like coffee with milk. Samuel was slightly darker, like a perfectly browned cake fresh from the oven. Mack mirrored his brother. And William, darkest and tallest of all, had skin the hue of rich molasses.

The men heard the commotion through the screen door shielding the indoors from the endless flies and bees of summer. "Well, seems like they're back," came from Jim.

"I reckon so," William said, head cocked, listening to the women inside.

"You know those hens are pecking about the girl," said Sam. The men all laughed in agreement. Anna Mary didn't stand a chance of being left alone now. Not with all those aunts about. Yes, Anna Mary would be fine now she was home. She was with the women. No one would ever cross one of them, thought each man. Not even her father.

Each man, lost in his own personal reflection, looked up as the screen door closed with a clang. Clint Joseph Lester emerged from the house with a beer in hand. In unspoken agreement, the men shifted, making room for him around the ice cream maker. The men all wore crisp, ironed slacks with short-sleeved, button-down shirts. Each wore a wedding ring, proud to state he was taken.

"Hello, boys," Clint—CJ to his friends—called out to the men. "How's that ice cream coming along?" He knew from experience ice cream took hours of turning the crank by hand, replacing ice and rock salt as needed to keep the cylinder cold enough for the cream to freeze. From the look of it, the men had been at the task for some time. CJ gazed out into his backyard, filled with children playing jump rope and tag. Mac's boys were climbing the lemon tree and tossing down ripened fruit. He smiled. He looked about for his grandson, nearly three, realizing he was likely penned inside the breakfast area of the kitchen with the other wee ones.

The men avoided verbalizing the obvious about their niece. They all knew the baby was his. They were angered they could do nothing. Mack, William, and Samuel had offered their solution to the problem to their sister Laura, and she was adamant they leave her husband be. To these proud men, who were protective of their own, why their sister stood by this good-for-nothing son of a gun made no sense. Sounds of women's laughter wafted into the yard, easing the tension between the men.

CJ watched the men before him. He knew how they felt about him, and he didn't care. This was his home. His family. Nobody would mess with him. "Food sure smells good."

"Um-hum," came the response. Suddenly the back door opened, and the melodious voice of Annie Eastman filled the air. "Come on in, y'all. Supper's ready. Make those kids wash they hands before they come in."

The house was full. Everyone gathered in a loose circle as Samuel said the prayer. Prayer before meals was commonplace. No one would dare eat without giving the blessing. The Eastman and the Lester family was all about acknowledging the presence of the Lord.

There was a moment of uncertainty as to who would give the blessing. It was well known that CJ did not attend church. However, this was his home. Samuel looked to CJ across the room, his eyes asking, "Well?" CJ nodded to his brother-in-law, deferring, allowing him to give forth the blessing.

Everyone quieted. There was the wiggling and jostling for space of the young ones, but with a stern look they too settled. Samuel took in the room and all its occupants. They were gathered to celebrate the newest arrival to the family. He scanned the room, finding his niece and new grand niece. Clearing his voice, he began.

"Thank you, Lord, for giving us the opportunity to come together. Thank you, Lord, for letting our great family grow.

Thank you, Lord, for blessing our families with your love. And thank you, Lord, for the bounty of this meal we are blessed to have. Protect this new life, Lord, so she may grow to know, follow, and embrace you. Bless the women who prepared this feast and may we all give thanks to you and your greatness. In Jesus' name, Amen." A round of Amens followed.

Then began the well-practiced dance of dishing out plates. First came the men, then the smallest children who were placed in the shade of the back porch on a blanket that would be shaken out after they were all done eating. Next came the older children who took their plates and headed back outdoors to the many picnic tables. After the children were served, the women had their turn. First Anna Mary, then the other women served themselves and settled down to eating and talking.

Anna Mary sat numbly watching, yet not. She let the plate of food sit on her lap untouched. She was more concerned with the infant now sleeping in her grandmother's arms. Big Mama looked peaceful, Anna Mary thought. She didn't seem upset about the strange child. Big Mama instead slept like the child in her arms. Once more the question, Why me? entered Anna Mary's mind. What had she done to deserve this punishment, for the baby was punishment.

Daddy had told her she was his special girl. He told her because he loved her she had to give him what he wanted. He'd wanted her, had taken her, her innocence, her girlhood, her virginity. Her father had caused this child. Had Anna Mary been strong enough to stop her father entering her room whenever he

19

pleased, she'd not have this baby. For this wasn't the first time there had been a baby. She'd had her first child, Greg, at 15. Two years later, when the family was still in Oregon, Anna Mary had borne another child from her father. The child had been quietly given to a couple who couldn't have children. The whole affair was kept quiet. Yet here she was again with another baby from her father.

Anna Mary opened her eyes as she felt someone lift the plate from her legs. She'd not realized she'd even closed them. Thanking her Aunt, Anna Mary moved to get up. She needed to go upstairs. She needed some space, time alone. But getting up wasn't as easy as she'd thought. Her body was heavy with fatigue, breasts swollen with milk. Milk, she thought, oh, yes, the baby has to nurse.

"Let me get your father," Anna Mary heard her mother say.

"No, no, that's alright, Mama. I can make it." The last person she wanted was her father. He had done enough. There was well-orchestrated commotion. The coffee table moved back, and Aunts Rose and Verda were at her side. Each one took an arm, guiding their niece toward the staircase. Behind them, Laura rose to gather up the newborn.

"Now you sit, Laura," she heard her mother-in-law say. Laura was unaccustomed to being told what to do in her own home. Yet, as she looked into the eyes of Mother Dear, she knew she had no choice but to listen.

"Annie, come take the baby up, why don't you?" Annie Eastman, who had married into the family, was grateful for the chance to leave the room. She was a quiet, gentle woman who could sense conflict three miles away. Annie went to Mother Dear and gently took the soft, sweet-smelling new baby from her arms.

"Now you and Rose stay up with the girl. Send Verda back down now, you hear?" This was spoken nearly in a whisper.

"Yes, Mother," whispered Annie in response.

The room suddenly was too quiet. The women sensed the storm was coming. Some began to gather up plates and glasses, Laura among them. She wanted her husband. She wanted to be in her kitchen. She wanted to be anywhere but here.

"Leave those things be, gals," Mother Dear said. She had been waiting for months to have this conversation, and today she would be heard. The remaining women—her daughters Jessie Mae and Verda, her daughter-in-law Laura, and Laura's sisters, Louise and Lillie Mae—sat.

"I know my son done hurt that girl," she began. Everyone knew he'd harmed the girl. It was the open secret, the truth nobody talked about. Well, today there would be talk. "This has got to stop, Laura. You hear me? This has got to stop. It's wrong. He is her father. You are his wife." This last statement Mother Dear said with fierceness. "I know how men are. They want to stake claim wherever them think they can. She don't belong to him, you hear me?" Dear pointed her finger at her daughter-in-law whose cheeks were getting flushed. "Now you can get as mad as you want to, but I'm telling you the truth and you know it."

Laura found herself standing up. She was shaking with rage and embarrassment, but mostly rage. Who was this woman, mother of her husband or no, to tell her what to do? Of course she knew the woman was speaking the truth. But why in God's name did she have to do so in front of everyone! "Mother," she began, "I think this is between Clint and me."

No sooner were the words out of her mouth than was Mother Dear standing before her. "It is your business if you can handle it. Clearly you can't, because if you could handle your business my granddaughter wouldn't be upstairs feeding your bastard granddaughter. Don't you think I know, gal? I do know. My husband wasn't no different. He was a womanizer. He had children with other women. But never did he touch one of my girls. I'd have killed him. You don't ever let nobody . . . and I mean nobody . . . hurt your babies. I don't care how good what he has in his pants is. That is your baby upstairs, Laura D. Now what she gone do with not one but two babies that look as different as night and day? The best thing you can do is get her married off as soon as possible."

Mother Dear sat back in her chair, shaking her head in disgust. "Now don't think I'm just talking to her," she said to the other women. "This goes for all y'all."

This was too much for Laura. She rose to her feet, thinking to let Mother Dear know . . . something. She was so upset she was seeing splotches of light through her eyes. Yet she didn't speak. Instead, she was pulled back onto the sofa by warm, careful hands. Someone stroked her back, attempting to calm her. Laura did not want to be calm. She wanted to get these people out of her house, starting with Mother Dear. She wanted to go see about her daughter and new granddaughter.

Laura did none of these things. She simply sat, taking in the words of her mother-in-law.

Clearly this is my story of how the family dealt with my arrival. I believe it was probably more like this than I want to admit. This is how the Lester women were, direct and to the point. The Eastman women, on the other hand, were what we called church women. They had comments, for sure, but the comments were masked or filtered through Bible verses and exaltations thanking their Lord for one thing or another. As a little girl, I preferred the Lester aunts to the Eastman aunts. The Lester women were fun, spirited, knew how to enjoy themselves, and knew how to talk and did so with abandon.

ALONE

I like sitting in Mama's bedroom. This room is darker than mine. Mama likes the shades drawn, especially during the day. The room stays cooler, she always explains when I ask. I sit on the queen-sized bed, my feet not quite touching the floor, watching yet not watching the television. Speed Racer is on, which is okay, but really not that interesting. I like Kimba the White Lion better. I used to like Casper, but ever since I started school kids call me Casper, the unfriendly ghost. So I don't watch Casper anymore. Alone, I sit on the edge of the bed to be as close to the TV set as I want to without fear of being reprimanded. Besides today Mama has company, Miss Linnie.

I like to watch the shadows on the wall. Sometimes I'm so close, trying to make out the shadow's shapes, that I leave a nose smudge. I place my small, six-year-old hand close to the wall and make rabbit shapes with my fingers. Bored with this game, I move around the bed to the mirrored dresser. It is the low, long kind with nine drawers in rows of three. I think of ways to count the same nine drawers each time I come into Mama's room—three down, three across, three diagonal. Just like tic tac toe. AVON creams in small pink and orange jars, nail polish bottles with white, pointed caps clutter on a corner of the dresser top along with two containers of talcum powder. I wake early each morning to watch Mama coat her honey brown body with the white powder to keep cool during the hot summer days while she worked at the post office.

Looking into the framed mirror, I smile. In a whisper I say, "I am pretty. Mama told me so." It doesn't matter that at school kids called me names or said I had cooties. Reaching up, I touch my eyelashes. If only I could see them. I stand on tiptoe to see my eyes better in the dresser mirror. Everyone says my eyes are pink. I cannot tell for sure, but I had to believe what I'd been told about myself. Wiping the mirror clean of its breath-imposed fog with my long, thick ponytail, I gaze more intently.

There is no one else who looks like me. Albino. I am Albino. I remember hearing two teachers talking before school was out. They had been talking about me. Saying how relieved they were to not have me in their classroom. A-L-B-I-N-O. Mrs. F had told me there were other Albino people, but I only knew me. My hair feels like cotton candy, just not pink. My eyelashes tickle my fingers when I touch them, and when I squeeze my arm it turns pink, then fades back to white. No, there is no one else like me. I wonder if Kimba the White Lion ever had to stay out of the sun. On the cartoon, it didn't look like it. Maybe albino lions were different.

Most of the time I feel ugly. A white blob. The Pillsbury Dough Boy changed into a girl. I try to make myself invisible. I long to have brown skin like everybody else in the family. I imagine one morning I will wake up with skin the same honey brown as Mama. Yet each day I wake up with the same pinkish white skin.

I know I shouldn't touch the necklaces, bracelets, and earrings on the dresser, but I do it anyway, with delicate fingers. I very much want to wear the blue and green beaded necklace my fingers trace. I glance at the door. Safe. No one coming. I take the shiny beads from Mama's jewelry box, placing them around my neck. I am beautiful. I want to run into the living room to show Mama and Miss Linnie, but I can't. I'll get into big trouble. I am supposed to be playing quietly. But what I really want is to play outside with all the other kids. I remove the beads, placing them exactly where I'd found them. Wiping my nose on the hem of my yellow sundress, I listen to the grownups' laughter from the other room. There are more than two voices. There is more company. When had that happened?

I walk to the bedroom door and peek into the living room. Empty. Everyone is in the kitchen, playing cards.

"Three low," says Miss Linnie.

"Five low. We can do that, can't we, Tookas?"

"Sure, baby," I hear Mama say.

Daddy Bob is there. I am excited to hear his voice. He is the only person that calls Mama Tookas. He isn't my real father, but Daddy Bob acts like he's our Daddy. Whenever he comes, he brings presents and hugs and kisses and stories from all over. The last time he'd come he'd brought pineapple from Hawaii. We could hardly believe that the brown prickly fruit had a yellow inside that tasted so good. I liked the way the fruit tasted, tangy and sweet. I feel a little safer knowing Daddy Bob is there. Mama wouldn't even think of yelling at me now. Mama liked to be in a good mood for him.

I ignore the loud beating of my heart and take slow, deliberate steps through the living room to the door of the kitchen. At first no one notices me. I watch four people sitting around the breakfast table playing Bid Whist. A man I don't know sits at the table. He's White. We don't know any White people. No longer afraid of interrupting, I'm curious about the man. He even knows how to play cards. He sits in the chair facing the open door, facing me, laughing easily. He must be a friend of Daddy Bob's from the Navy, otherwise he wouldn't be sitting in Mama's kitchen acting like he belongs there. I shyly tiptoe over to the chair where Mama sits.

"Mama, can I go outside, please?"

The sun is shining, and I know it's hot, but I want to go out anyway. I wait, hoping to hear a yes. I look at Daddy Bob for support. He motions for me to come closer to him. I do so, receiving a gin-scented kiss on my cheek. Wrinkling my face at the smell, Daddy Bob laughs, lifting me onto his lap. I can feel his scratchy, unshaven face against my smooth cheek as he hugs me close. Feeling perfectly safe, I regard my mother.

Mama sighs. They play out the hand with me sitting on Daddy Bob's lap. This will pacify me for a bit longer. After the hand is over, Mama suggests that everyone stretch. She takes me from Bob's lap and carries me back to my bedroom. "Now, baby, I know you want to go out and play, but Mama can't let you do that. I'm afraid you'll get sick. Remember the last time we let you play outdoors when it was warm?"

I nod my head nod against her shoulder. "You got really sick and threw up. You had such a bad sunburn, you cried." She watches my lip tremble. She shares my conviction that this was not fair. She holds me on her lap and looks out the open window. Sunshine streams into the small bedroom. Why she put the girls in a room where two walls were windows she'd never know.

Straightening my back, I tell myself I will not cry, not in front of Mama anyway. Doing so would only make her angry. I hug Mama and slide from her lap. I sit on the floor in front of the bookshelf, my back to mother.

"Now, you just play here like Mama's special girl, okay? You can watch the sun go down soon. If it cools off near dusk, perhaps you can go into the backyard with your brother and sister." My mother pats my shoulder before leaving the room to rejoin the card game that calls her name.

I sit, unmoving like a statue. Then I stand, going to my bed so I can see into the backyard. The sun warms me through the closed window. Soon my throat tightens. I try to hold in my tears, but I can't. The sobs win out, leaving my throat heaving in big spurts. I cover my mouth so no one can hear. Curling into a ball, my body shakes with each muffled cry. Salt-tinged tears sting my eyes and cheeks. I never see the setting of the sun.

JUST ONE OF US KIDS

To my nieces and nephews, especially the older ones, I have always just been Auntie. To them, I am no different than my sister. If anything, they have grown to be protective of me, like my brothers and sister. Everyone learned early on to be mindful of me. "Watch out for your sister," was often heard by us all as we left our house to play outdoors.

One summer when we were all under twelve our family lived in what we later would come to know was subsidized housing. We lived in an apartment complex consisting of ten units. Six on one side, and four on the other. There were ten families living there, which meant there were lots of kids to play with. I was sitting in the shade watching my brother Greg and a group of kids play baseball. A huge parking area had been cleared of cars to let the kids play without worry of someone smashing a car window. I wasn't happy having to sit in the shade. I hugged my knees, resting my chin on them while listening to the kids with my eyes closed. Lost in my own world of sulking, I almost

31

missed my name being called. Greg was calling me. Looking up, I yelled, "What?"

My brother Greg was the biggest, baddest boy in the complex. He was usually a team captain at whatever sport or hide-and-seek or tug of war game was at play. Squinting, I looked up at him as he grabbed my hand, pulling me into the parking lot turned baseball diamond. I went along because, for one, he had my arm, so I had no choice, and, for two, if I didn't he'd get mad at me. Plus, I was curious.

"Y'all, today Natalie gets to play with us. Whose team she gonna be on?" I looked around at all the kids now gathered in a circle around us. A few kids groaned at having to let me play with them.

"She can't even see, man," Stevie said.

"So what?" Greg yelled in a burst of anger. "Today, she plays. Just for that, she's on your team."

Taking me aside, he said, "Now, try to hit the ball. I'll tell you when to swing. Okay?"

Nodding my head, I couldn't believe what was happening. I was terrified. I was excited. I knew this was a bad idea, but at least I was getting to play, and our mother couldn't see us from our apartment balcony. Why not?

When it was my turn at bat, the kid who was pitcher, Claudine, came right up close to pitch.

"Easy out," somebody said and snickered. My cheeks burned with shame because I knew he was right. Holding the wooden bat like I saw the others do, I waited for the pitch.

"Swing!" Greg yelled.

Strike one. Face burning, I was determined to hit the ball. Claudine pitched again, and I swung.

Strike two. Heart pounding, I knew I would strike out for certain.

"Time out!" Stevie called. Everybody gathered around again. "Look, we know she can't see, so . . . ," he paused, looking at Greg, "let's give her more chances to hit the ball. Just this once."

I listened, head bowed. I kept my head down, not wanting to meet the eyes of anyone.

Greg yelled out, "Yeah! Y'all know she can't see, not like us anyway. Nine strikes. Nine chances she gets to hit the ball. Awright." It was not a question.

Moments before, I had been the dreaded addition to the team, and now I was getting nine tries to hit the ball. I couldn't believe it. So back to bat I went. Now everyone was telling me when to swing the bat. Everyone was cheering me on. With each pitch, Claudine moved closer to me, lightly tossing the ball my way. Concentrating on the eighth pitch, I heard the bat connect with the ball.

"Run! Run! Run!" all the kids yelled. Greg ran beside me, telling me where the bases were. I made it to second base where I had to stay. Almost out of breath, I bent over, looking at the ground. I was on second base. I had hit the ball! Me! Then I heard the bat crack again, sending the ball out into the street. Again, Greg ran alongside me as I rounded onto third base, then making it back to home. I was jumping up and down so hard my braids were hitting the side of my face. I didn't care. I looked over to where I had been sitting in the shade, and the stoop was filled with grownups. They were laughing and cheering right along with us. When our team went back outfield I didn't know what to do. Grabbing my hand, Stevie led me to the side of our playing field.

"Stand here," he said. "Stand in the shade. Your mama is watching, and I don't want her to yell at you."

My head turned to and fro, looking for her. Would she be angry?

"Don't worry," he said. "It's okay. If a ball comes your way, we'll tell you to duck."

I stood in the shade of a birch tree in the outfield until the inning was over. Afterward, I walked toward Greg.

"You did alright. You cool. Now go sit on the stoop in the shade before Mama gets mad."

Once more I sat perched on the stoop, my chin resting on my knees. I was so happy. I played the scene of me running to the bases over and over in my head. I had played baseball, and I had hit the ball. Thanks to my brother, I had been included.

My brother Greg was good for creating opportunities like that, to prove I was one of the kids. He found ways to let me fend for myself without getting myself killed or seriously hurt. The year I was ten and he thirteen and Felecia eight, we had gotten bikes for Christmas. Mama spent a lot of time outside with us helping Felecia and I learn to ride our bicycles. Mine was a red stingray bike with a white seat. It had red, white, and blue tassels that streamed from the handle bars. I loved that thing. By spring, we were all masters of cycling.

One Saturday, after being hounded by us all, especially Greg, Mama relented and let us ride our bikes from our house to our grandparents' house, which was twenty blocks away. We listened to the standard words of caution we were always given. "Watch your sister, Felecia. Listen to Greg, and for god's sake, don't get hit."

We three stood somberly, promising to ride carefully and to listen to each other and to call when we arrived at Grandmother and Granddaddy's house. Four blocks away from home, my brother rode up beside me. "Just so you know," he said, "I'm not watching you. You're on your own."

"I'm gonna tell Mama!" Felecia called out.

"Shut up, Lisa," Greg said without looking at her. "If you tell, you will never get to do this again, so shut up."

We rode the next eight blocks to 82nd Avenue, which was a major, busy street. Greg had gotten there first. He guided us across the intersection, then took off on his blue five-speed. Felecia and I looked at each other and followed after him. We crossed 73rd Avenue, which was only a two-lane street then. Putting our bikes in the backyard, we sat on the back steps, breathless. We made it to our grandparents' home in no time. I had managed to get there without incident. We had a pact to not tell anyone what we had done. We had made the ride and would do so again many times before we ultimately moved to the Holly Street house. True to his word, my brother hadn't really looked after me. He let me experience the feeling of riding for myself. I got to feel my heart pound with the uncertainty of whether or not I would fail. He let me fly.

When we were teenagers, it was Greg who once again pushed for me to be able to join him in some fun. He was allowed to have a sixteenth birthday party on the lower level of our house. Our mom had said I was too young to go to the party. Greg was the one who promised to look out for me at his party. That night I danced, laughed, and had fun with his friends. I had been allowed to dress up in my bell-bottom jeans and my pink, sparkly top. Every so often I would see him watching me, checking out who I was dancing with. One boy asked me to slow dance. I was eager to do so since I had only heard about slow dancing. Dennis and I were making our way to the makeshift dance floor when we were stopped. "No slow dancing with my little sister, man. She don't do that yet."

Angry and embarrassed, I fled outside. I knew he was only looking out for me, but I didn't, in this case, want him to. My cheeks were the same color of my shirt, I just knew it. I leaned against the side of the house, trying to breathe. I never get to do anything, I silently fumed.

Dennis dropped his interest in me. He told me I was bad news, off limits, and just not worth dealing with my brother. After calming down, I went back into the party and saw for myself what slow dancing truly was. The couples looked like they were stuck together. I watched Dennis dance with another girl. His hands were all over her. Eeww, I definitely did not want to have someone on me like that. No, not slow dancing, at all. Those kids were three years older than I was and knew things I did not yet know. I would have preferred to have decided for myself, but as I observed the boys grinding on the girls I was disgusted. Yet again, Greg had watched out for me.

My brother was one of the few people in our family who just accepted me for who I was. He was my protector, as well as my tormentor. He used to tell me that I was found left in a basket on the front porch, which was why I didn't look like anybody in the family. I remember crying the first dozen or so times he said this. I was a slow learner. My feelings were so hurt. All I wanted was to belong, to know that I too had a place in our home. I didn't want to be a charity case. I would cry so hard, my face would be swollen from the tears. In the end, he would always say, "You know I'm just kidding you. Right, sis?"

But I didn't really know for certain. I think he grew bored of this game and finally laid off of me. Maybe he just got tired of the crying. Either way, I was relieved.

By the time we reached high school, it became automatic that if anyone bothered me I would let Greg know. I only had to do this my first year. I recall sitting in the lunchroom alone because I had no friends. Someone threw food at me. No matter how I ducked or dodged from side to side, bread and vegetables landed against my back or in my hair. I could not tell who was doing this to me and began to cry. Abandoning my tray, I went down behind the swimming pool where I knew my brother would be. He and his friends smoked down there. He took one look at me, then pushed away from the wall of the building, angry.

"Stop crying and tell me what happened."

Sniffling, I related to him what had occurred in the lunchroom.

"Just go back," he said. "I will follow you. I don't want them to know I'm with you. I'll watch you." Of course I did what he told me to. I went back to the table, avoiding the bits of food on the bench. Not long after I sat, yet again food came flying my way.

At once there was a commotion. I turned around to see my brother punching a boy. The boy who had been tormenting me. Greg's friends pulled him from the boy as the vice principal came strolling in. I rose from the table as the vice principal took my brother by the arm. I followed behind them as they headed to the office. Greg told me to go to class, so did the vice principal. I didn't. I wasn't going to let Greg be punished for protecting me. I sat on a bench in the outer office while Greg was being lectured. I asked the secretary if I could call our mom. She relented, inviting me behind the ever long counter that divided the administration from the students.

Mama worked in Berkeley at the police department. I wasn't sure she would be available. She was. I told her in a rush what happened. At her request, I handed the telephone to a secretary. Less than a half hour later, Mama was there.

The school hated my mother. This had been the case when I was in junior high and now here. Mama took me by the hand as she walked into the office where Greg was being held. We, Greg and I, sat, silently watching our mother give the vice principal a piece of her mind. To his credit, the man looked Mama directly in the eye. He sat on the edge of his desk, arms folded across his chest, waiting. We knew what she was capable of. We knew Mama would defend her children to the death. If afterward she discovered we weren't telling the truth, all hell would break loose. So, we had learned not to lie where school was concerned.

"Since you people clearly cannot control your students, and since you allow them to throw food at my daughter, then my son has no choice but to defend his sister. Wouldn't you agree, Mr. Johnston?" Mama did not sit. She stood facing the man who knew by looking at us that he was out of his league when it came to reasoning with our parent. I watched him nod his head in agreement.

"Of course a brother looks to his sister's safety. However, Mrs. Young—"

"I'm glad we agree, Mr. Johnston. Of course, my son will not be reprimanded, and this matter will not go in either of their records."

Mr. Johnston nodded.

"Now as for the boy who harassed my daughter . . . " Mama paused, giving the poor man before her the chance to come up with his own idea. She of course was fully in charge of the situation.

"He will be suspended for three days, and I will notify his parents." He was sweating. I think he would have agreed to nearly anything if only to get her out of his office.

Mr. Johnston rose, hand extended to Mama, believing he was done with the uncomfortable exchange. We did not move. We knew better. She did not take his hand. "Please know, Sir, my daughter will let me know if anything further happens to her."

Again he glanced at us. I imagined he was thinking, I have this girl for three years. Good God Almighty. "Of course, Mrs. Young. I have no doubt she will indeed let you know. Thank you for coming. I wish all parents were so, um, involved."

Mother had turned away, beckoning us with a tilt of her head to follow her out.

"Go get your books. We are going home." This was not easy, as the hall was filled with students trying to get a look through the square glass window into the office. Word had spread that my brother was in there. A lot of people had seen him punch the boy bullying me. As security cleared the hall, we joined the crowd of curious students, clearing a path now for our walk to our lockers. In a feat of stunning stupidity, Greg called out in a clear, deep baritone voice, "This is my little sister. You mess with her, you mess with me."

I thought Mama was going to pop him on the head, but she didn't. Walking between us, she led our exit from the building.

"Why did you just say that?" I asked, wanting to know because in my mind I had just become a big bullseye. No answer. I wanted to ask again, but Mama's "Enough" made my lips close tight.

In the car, I sat in back while Greg rode shotgun, which was fine with me as no one was talking anyway. After a few minutes, Mama asked us what happened. I started to talk, but Greg cut me off.

"This boy was throwing food at Natalie, Mama. He thought it was funny. It wasn't funny. Food was all over her back and in her hair." I squeezed into the corner of the backseat directly behind Mama. I did not want to feel her eyes on me. Just by her sigh I could tell she was clenching the steering wheel. She always did that when she drove and was angry.

"You were there?"

"Well, not at first. But I saw him do it. I did."

I was barely breathing. Greg was telling the truth. So why was I not breathing? I don't really know. I was just terrified that . . . well, that maybe Mama would say it was my fault.

"Natalie came and found me."

"Well?" Mama said, the question directed at me.

I related what had occurred. Starting with getting my food and sitting by myself at a table. The feeling of food hitting me and doing my best to avoid it. "Finally, I went to find Greg. He was down by the pool." I left out the smoking part. "He told me to stop crying and to go back and he would follow me. He watched the boy throw food. The next thing I knew, Greg was punching him. He told the boy to leave me alone. Then they took him to the vice principal's office. So I went too."

"I didn't think Greg should get in trouble for trying to take care of me."

Greg and I hadn't been in the same school since elementary. This would be the only year we were in high school together because he was a senior. By now my brother didn't need to be told to watch out for me. He just did. It was the end of

September. School had only been in session for three weeks. I didn't want to go through the whole year scared for my life. I was a brainy kid who didn't look like everyone else and who loved books. Having Albinism made me stand out like a sore thumb. I didn't want high school to be like what I'd endured at my last school. There I'd been targeted as not Black, which was stupid because I was Black. I'd been beaten so severely I'd been taken to the hospital. I had been kicked, leaving me with bruised ribs. Punched, my nose bloodied. Bruises on my face, arms, and legs. I had been traumatized. I stayed home for two weeks. When I did return to school, I was terror stricken. My classes had been moved so I was in the main building instead of in the portables. The teachers and administration did their best to buffer me from teasing. No matter, teasing still took place daily. No, I did not want to ever have to go through that again.

Once again silence filled the car. "You both did the right thing," said Mama.

Greg looked back at me, a wide grin filling his face.

"Going forward . . . "

Here we go, I thought. What must I do differently? I dreaded this question. Mama always asked us this after any sort of incident. It hadn't even been my fault.

"Going forward, Gregory, you have my permission to whip anybody's ass who hurts your sister."

"What? Huh?" came from us in surprise.

"I'm sick and tired of you being afraid. It's not right or fair or acceptable."

Had I just heard Mama give my brother permission to fight on my behalf? Yes, I had. Wow.

"The key is . . . ," she had stopped at a red light, "don't get caught." We all laughed.

Mama then launched into a tale of how she as a little girl had had to fight the battles of one of her male cousins. "He was a boaster. He never knew when to just shut up and walk away. No, he was always getting beaten up. He would come to me, and I was a year younger than him, mind you. And I would go beat the boy to a pulp. I never was caught, though. I mean, how could I . . . a nice girl . . . beat up a boy older than me?"

Man, Greg and I laughed about that even after we grew up. Just don't get caught.

Mama assured me I would make friends, and, of course she was right. I did. There were no more food throwing incidents. No one bothered me at all. Mama didn't have to return to the school on my behalf again that year.

The other thing that had occurred was my brother's friends would come up to me then and again to see if I was alright. These boys were the ones who mostly didn't care about going to class. They cared about hanging out together. Slowly I formed friendships. By the time Gregory finished high school, I was just fine.

Inasmuch as my brother was my chief protector and tormentor, I too was his. I would be remiss if I led you to believe that I was the perfect angel in our relationship. Greg was my brother, and we fought. Greg was also my hero.

When I was two years old, I covered myself with dirt and mud so I could look like him. He was dark like chocolate. I'm told we were both excited at our dirt and mud discovery. Sadly, with a good bath, my brown disappeared. When he went off to school, I was devastated. My number one playmaker was gone. Plus, he got to do homework. I was fascinated. Daily after school, our Aunt Diane would sit with us at the kitchen table helping Greg with his homework. By the time I reached kindergarten, not only could I identify my colors and numbers, I could read.

Greg had one challenge, which followed him always. It only happened when he became excited or was frustrated or angry. He stuttered. Few boys teased him, though. They'd learned early on not to tease Greg, because my brother had a temper and would just punch anyone who gave him cause. Kids learn pretty quickly about character. Mama was always cautioning Greg to slow down when he spoke so that he wouldn't stutter. This worked at home, but at school things were altogether different.

Greg was in what we kids called the special class. Classrooms meant for children with behavior issues or who were just a little behind their peers in the other classrooms. Usually the two issues went hand in hand. We were separated grade-wise by three years. That being said, by the time I was in second grade I was reading his books and helping him practice reading aloud. After school, we would sit at the dining room table, both with our schoolbooks out. Homework was serious business. We did what we could to get done quickly so we could go outside. Our mother knew the doings of children. She made us work longer. We had to do our math out loud, spell vocabulary words again and again to her satisfaction, and, yes, read out loud. While this was easy for me, they were daunting for my big brother. So, when Mama wasn't looking I would help him. We would sit on the floor in his room some evenings, where I would help him sound out words. We had reading books, similar to the Dick and Jane readers of the lower grades. Some of the kids in my class were still reading Dick and Jane.

My way of getting back at Greg when I tired of being teased was to call him names. I would use words like, "You're an imbecile," rather than calling him stupid outright. His face would nearly turn purple with rage. He might not know what I was saying, but Greg knew it wasn't nice.

More than anything, we were a team. We kept our younger sister and brother in line. We had a pact when it came to getting time away from home on Saturday afternoons. After chores were done and groceries put away and if Mama was in a good mood, we would be allowed to do what we pleased. I was allowed to take the bus to the main branch of our library alone when I turned twelve. This meant I was no longer relegated to the children's room. This meant too that I could read what I wanted without having to ask for books from behind the librarian's checkout counter.

So, if I had free time I could usually be found at the library. My brother was almost 16 by then and only had time for his friends. I didn't really know what they did, and honestly I didn't much care. Anyway, time to ourselves was rare. Saturday afternoons typically meant each of us had to take one of the younger ones with us. We hated having them encroach on our time. Plus, it meant if we decided to do something we weren't supposed to then we had to bribe them not to tell. Bribery was tricky. It didn't always work.

One Saturday Greg was supposed to take Felecia with him. I knew he had a girlfriend who lived near my school. They liked to go to the park to make out. Greg had given Felecia money for the ice cream truck with the understanding she wouldn't tell Mama about him having a girlfriend. With great gusto, Felecia told our mother about Greg making out with his girlfriend. He was so mad. After enduring the lecture from hell, we did our best to convince Mama to let Felecia just play on our block and we would alternate taking Clinton.

I would cover for Greg. Cover as in back up his story when we both knew he was lying. It was in my best interest. I knew if I colluded with him in front of our mother I could at a later time call in a favor. Though I never did.

Neither of us had any way of predicting our close bond would sever within the next two years.

LIFE AT SCHOOL

Elementary school was my favorite. After we moved and I began to attend E. Morris Cox School, I slowly made friends. I remember knowing most all the teachers. At first I would walk down the hall to my classroom as close to the wall as possible so I could look or at least listen in on the other rooms. I was curious about what the other kids were learning. Usually the teachers would wave or say hello. By the time I moved into the second building in fifth grade, I had several friends. Mrs. Finnafoss would come twice a week by then to help me with my schoolwork. I always finished my work quickly so I learned how to type on an old Smith-Corona typewriter. I was intrigued with how the metal keys felt. My fingers would stroke each row, feeling the cool smoothness of the keys. Fascinated, I would watch the long metal arms attached to each key strike the paper and a letter would appear. How was this possible? When I was alone, I would carefully raise one of the arms to feel its texture. I knew this was sort of how words were printed in books but somehow different. I imagined the typewriters that were used to make the large print books I used were humungous. I would never see one of these machines, though over time my books would become smaller in size while still having the larger print that I loved.

My life changed significantly in the fall of 1974. I completed sixth grade and was promoted to junior high school. We moved from our subsidized apartment to a house. Mama's parents had given their daughter their old house, moving themselves into the biggest house I had ever seen in the Oakland hills.

So I began junior high. Elementary school was my best experience, and junior high school was by far the worst nightmare. Like everyone else there, I went from a welcoming school to a new one filled with lots of kids, a whole myriad of buildings, and new expectations.

I felt lost there, and often I was truly lost. The main building had two floors of classrooms, which I learned to navigate quickly enough by falling back on counting doors. The whole locker situation was excruciating. There were combination locks with really tiny numbers, and there was a formula to making them work that was beyond me because I couldn't read the numbers. Thankfully there was always somebody I could ask for help.

The portables were also confusing, and there were a lot of them. I think I spent the entire first semester lost in the portables. They were clumped together in large groups. There was the group of twelve that were adjacent to the main building, and then there was another group of nine or so located on the other side of the gym. Oh, and let's not even talk about the gym and PE. More on that later. During my first year, thankfully, I only had two classes in the portables, English and Art. The first being in the closer group of self-contained classrooms, and the second out of the schoolyard.

I also had teachers who were unfamiliar with my eyesight challenges, which was a source of constant anxiety. During this time, I met a new VH teacher (a visual specialist), Anita Ramage. She was completely different from Mrs. Finnafoss whom I had known for seven years. Mrs. Finnafoss retired when I finished sixth grade. She had waited, she told me, because she wanted to see me promoted. I think now she also wanted to see me through to the end as her last act of teaching. Mrs. Ramage was younger and had black hair. She also was more open about her life, sharing that she had a daughter who was a blind radio announcer. In the six years I would know Mrs. Ramage, I would learn lifelong skills. The most important of which was and continues to be to self-advocate.

Frick Junior High School was awful. I hated being there. I was teased so much each day that I lost count of the incidents. I learned through trial and error to become friends with the biggest, meanest girl in school. Like me, she had few friends and stuck out like a sore thumb, but she dealt with it differently. When people bothered Sharon, she pushed or punched them. So kids steered clear of her.

51

I approached her one day in the lunchroom that also served as the school auditorium, and I asked her shyly if she would be my friend. After that, I began to have a different existence. Until then, I had been the brunt of jokes about my mother having had relations with a White man or a milkman or Casper's father. I had been intentionally tripped, intimidated, and had food thrown at me in the lunchroom. I wasn't used to being treated this way. So I finally asked Big Sharon to be my friend. She looked at me like I was crazy. I guess she didn't get many requests to be friends.

So we became friends. The next time someone chose to throw food at me they were punched by Sharon who let the entire lunchroom know that I was "her" friend and anyone who messed with me would have to deal with her. While I was proud and grateful to be defended by her, I worried there would be retaliation. And, of course, there was.

A week later I was ambushed on my way home by a girl and an entire group of kids calling for a fight. I was on the losing end of an altercation that consisted of me being hit and kicked in the grocery store parking lot across the street from school. I was kept home the next day while my parents, by then divorced, stood as a united front for their children and met with school officials.

My parents were assured that the situation would not occur again. They were skeptical. I was sent to school the following day terrified at what might and could happen to me. I spent breaks either in the nurse's office or in the library. Given a choice, I preferred the latter. In the library I discovered the poetry of Phyllis

Wheatley, learned about the writings of Langston Hughes and Paul Lawrence Dunbar, discovered the Harlem Renaissance, and developed a love for encyclopedias.

Teachers, aware of the importance of keeping me safe, kept an eye on me. Somehow I managed to escape further physical harm, at least for another year. In the spring of 1976 there was a great deal of racial discord in Oakland. In my school, if your skin was not brown you were a target of bullying. I was aware that White students were being attacked just because of their skin color. Sadly, I too would fall prey to attack because of my fair skin.

One sunny afternoon while leaving the main building with hundreds of other students, I was pushed so hard I nearly fell out the door. Turning around to see who had pushed me, I realized I couldn't tell. I moved forward, now in the courtyard between the main building and the lunchroom/auditorium. I felt my loose hair yanked, causing me to cry out. Turning again, I was punched in the nose then slapped by oncoming hands I could not see. Falling to the ground, my hands covered my face filled with blood. I was kicked repeatedly. I could hear girls laughing, and all I could think was, I'm not White.

Oakland was a hotbed, fueled with racial unrest. I became its latest casualty. Eventually a school official intervened, scooping me up into his arms. I was carried to the nurse's office where an ambulance was called. By the time I reached the hospital, my parents were there. They were furious. I could hear my father trying to calm my mom. She was in tears. We both were.

Managing to escape any broken limbs, I was cleaned and bandaged up and taken home. The drive home was silent, save for me crying in the backseat. I was curled up into myself, only vaguely aware of the streets we passed on our way home. I knew these streets, having memorized them when I was little. Daddy took the MacArthur exit, drove by Mills College, went around the bend, crossed Seminary going down Camden street. We passed by the Evergreen Cemetery, just a short walk to my school. We crossed Foothill and Bancroft, then moved onto Havenscourt with its tree-lined sidewalks. We would be home in less than five minutes. I began to shake then. I closed my eyes. I think I believed that if I didn't look at my parents or my skinned hands or pay attention to the bandages on my face, the whole thing, the whole experience would continue to be unreal. But I could not ignore the soreness in my ribs and thighs where I'd been kicked. The bruises would later turn purple, then black, then that funny green, signifying healing.

Everyone on our street knew I had been attacked and were hanging out near our house when we arrived home. I was afraid and strangely embarrassed for having been beaten up and wouldn't look at anyone. There were questions I didn't want to answer again and again, and yet I had to. My mother wanted answers, and I repeated to her what had happened to me earlier that afternoon. Eventually Daddy took pity on me and called an end to the questioning, sending me to my room.

Unable to sleep, I lay in bed and took stock of all the places I hurt. My fingers traced my face, feeling the bruises and the swelling. Blood crusted on the outside of my nose. I would have a black eye. Maybe two. My lip was cracked. And that's just my face, I told myself. I didn't want to think about the rest of me. Hot tears fell, landing on my ears before becoming absorbed into my pillow. I tried to make sense of what happened. My only memory was of me saying, "I'm not White" to a girl I didn't know. Afterward I was on the ground, having been punched in the face, then kicked. The only practical thing I had done was to cover my head. Eventually I slept.

When I woke, the sun had set. I groaned in pain as I tried to sit up. I mentally counted the number of steps from my bed to the bathroom. Twenty-seven. Light was unnecessary as I knew the layout of the entire downstairs where Greg and I had our bedrooms. As the seconds passed, it was clear I couldn't move without help. Then I felt arms around me, helping me to stand.

"Sh-sh," said Mama. "We'll go slow."

I wasn't sure I wanted to see myself in the mirror, and yet I knew I had to look. I had to see how bad I looked. I knew from my earlier tracing of fingers I had bruises and cuts on my face. Mama sat me on the toilet, and I waited for her to clean my face. I was reminded of when I was small and she would clean up all my scrapes from falling. She didn't say much save for consoling me and reassuring me I would heal. The washcloth felt amazing. It was cool on my oh-so-hot face. Mama wasn't saying much, I realized, because she was crying. I felt one of her hot tears fall onto my hand. And just as I had when I was small, my fingers found her face. I could tell she had been crying a lot.

Her eyes were puffy. Our foreheads touched, and I whispered. "I'll try to be okay, Mama." I was far from okay.

I slept a lot the next several days. I knew, in part, I was sleeping because my body was healing. Also, I did not want to face the world.

When I was awake, I was jumpy. I was terrified. I wouldn't go to school. I wouldn't even go outside. My whole world had been turned upside down. I believed people would look at me and feel sorry for me. I did not want their pity. I read. Great Expectations, To Kill A Mockingbird, and The Bluest Eye. Mrs. Ramage had brought large print copies of the first two books and a magnifying glass to assist me with the third.

Everyone, well, the adults, all tried to get me to return to school. I, the most compliant of my mother's four children, had become defiant, refusing to return for fear of being attacked again. They understood these feelings and yet, as Mama put it, "Children must be in school. You are no exception."

For two weeks I remained at home. Mrs. Ramage came every other day bringing my schoolwork and staying with me for two hours to complete the assignments. During this time, I was constantly in fear. When the topic of returning to school was mentioned, I would shake uncontrollably often erupting in tears. Finally, I was told I had to return to school.

Two weeks after being attacked, I returned to school. My parents arranged to have me driven home from school each day by a teacher who had taught me in seventh grade. My first day back, my father drove me to school, accompanying me inside to my first class.

I loved my dad and was comforted by his presence. He was tall and outwardly quiet. He was as dark as I was fair, and he was my Dad. He built cars, and I was proud of him. After the morning break, he left, assuring me that I would be taken home after school and to wait in the office. In his absence, my anxiety returned. I had a breakdown. I walked the halls in fear of someone tripping me or opening their locker only to hit me in the face. My parents were phoned, and it was suggested strongly I consider changing schools. The school for the blind was brought up once more. Horrified, my parents and I leave.

I come to hate being Black. I beg to go to a White school where I would look more like everyone else. I stay in the same school, left to work through my terror and newfound internalized racism. Several times a day the halls filled with everyone during the short break between classes. I was terrified by so many people and would flatten myself against my locker until the mass of bodies passed by. By then all my classes were in the main building as going to the portables had been deemed inappropriate for me. It would be a few months before I felt confident enough to walk to and from school.

Looking back, I believe this is where the fear of my own race began. I remember thinking that I didn't want to be Black. I didn't want to be with people who would hurt me just because

I looked different. This internalized process would affect me for two decades.

My family didn't fall into this category because they loved me without condition. While my older brother might tell me I had been left in a basket on the front porch as a baby, by then I knew he was kidding. It was his way of poking fun. Attending predominantly Black-populated schools, I had no choice other than to make things work.

By the time I reached high school, I was a bit more comfortable in my skin. In the first year I met with the teasing and bullying I had come to know in junior high, however, I wasn't physically harmed. I managed to find a few friends, and I participated in school clubs, thereby creating more friendships. I continued to be shy in groups, yet I remained confident in my intellect. In a school of 2,000 teenagers I was just another girl who looked a little different. By then I had also begun coloring my hair. I shifted between a blond afro-wearing girl to a red-haired press and curl kind of girl.

During junior high school, my eyes were my archenemy. I hated them for not doing what I thought they should. I hated my eyes because they, along with my skin, made me stand out. I sat in the front row in all my classes in school, which proved useless because I still could not see the board. I listened intently in class. This is how I learned. I would listen to my teachers explain concepts and then memorize those concepts, getting extra help when their meanings eluded me.

I became my own personal conveyor of self-hatred. I wanted to be anywhere than in my own skin. I would wish for brown skin when I was alone. I would pray to God to let me wake up looking like my brothers and sister. This of course never happened.

SEARCHING FOR PRETTY

I scour photos of myself as a child. Who am I within this family I was born into? Where did I fit? In one group photograph taken at a family gathering, I stand smiling proudly amongst my cousins with our parents behind us. I am the lone pale figure. In another, taken at the same gathering, I am barely visible. I'm more of a whiteout, missing facial features. Still another photo, taken in our backyard, shows my sister Felecia, two years my junior and I wearing matching outfits with bell-bottom pants and sleeveless tops. I also have a white, cap-sleeved T-shirt beneath it to protect my shoulders. My siblings smile directly into the camera while I gaze at the ground because the sun hurts my eyes.

As a teenager I was convinced I'd been dropped into the hell of my life, convinced I had been abandoned, left in a basket on a doorstep like my older brother teased. Why else would I have the experiences I did? No one else shared my experience in the family. No one else was singled out in the same way. No one else looked like me.

One Saturday afternoon when I was thirteen, we kids were left at home while our mother went grocery shopping. She left us with our younger brother, the Baby as we referred to him. Our other name for him was Troublemaker because although he caused it, we always bore the brunt of responsibility for his antics. I had been left in charge, which really meant little. We all had chores to do, and we knew if the chores weren't done we would never hear the end of it. We were sixteen, thirteen, eleven, and six. Clinton kept going in and out of the backdoor, tracking dirt in. Greg grew madder and madder as he had to keep re-mopping the kitchen floor. After the third or fourth time of watching Clinton walk across the wet floor, with a smirk on his cherubic face because he knew what he was doing, we were all ready to kill him. Somebody got the idea of putting him in the living room without his shoes. He was put in charge of choosing cleaning music. We would have to listen to "Shining Star" by Earth, Wind & Fire a lot, but it was worth it. We would know where he was, and Greg would stop yelling. Plus, we could finally get finished with our cleaning chores.

We had a Saturday tradition in our house. We would wake to the smell of a hot breakfast, usually pancakes, bacon, and eggs, but sometimes there were grits instead of pancakes. If Mama was in a really good mood, Marvin Gaye would be playing upstairs where the main part of the house was.

Today had been a Marvin Gaye, "Let's Get It On" morning, which was the best kind of Saturday. Our house on Holly Street was two stories with internal back stairs off the laundry room, at the back of the kitchen connecting the two floors. Greg, Felecia, and I emerged from our bedrooms, sluggish and sleepy-eyed to the sunny yellow kitchen where breakfast was set out on the table. Mama was happy and chatty. When we were nearly done eating, she told us if we did our chores while she went out, when she returned, and the groceries were put away, we could do what we wanted.

Greg and I were the only ones this news really applied to. I knew he would vanish to hang out with his friends and our cousins Giles and Dwayne. I wanted to go to the main library downtown. Felecia and Clint were still too young to go any-where without Mama unless Greg and I were forced to have one of them tag along with us. I hoped today we wouldn't have to take them. I saw Greg was hoping for the same thing. Mama watched us eyeing one another. She knew how we felt. She also knew we wouldn't ask. We had no choice in the matter.

"You two can stop with the sidelong looks. You won't have to take your brother and sister with you today ... provided you get those chores done and put away the groceries."

You never saw two teenagers more eager to take on cleaning the house. Greg took the kitchen, which meant he did the dishes, swept, and mopped. Felecia cleaned the bathrooms, and I vac-uumed. We had to clean our own rooms. I also had to start laundry. Plus, I kept an eye on the younger two.

Within one hour of Mama leaving, the house was clean. Greg and I had places to go. Felecia just wanted to play outside, which she could do with no one watching her. With everything done, we settled on the carpet in the living room to watch Soul Train. We imitated the Soul Train Dancers with our own soul train line. We were having a good time. We heard Mama honk the horn, which meant we all had to help bring the food in. Once all bags were accounted for and unpacked, folded and put away, Greg and I made a beeline downstairs to get ready to go. I never made it out the kitchen, though.

Called into Mama's bedroom, which was right off the dining room, I saw bags and bags on her large bed. She had been to Pay 'n Save, which was the drugstore and everything store up at The Mall on 73rd and Bancroft. I wondered what all the bags contained. Mama was going on and on about something. I hadn't really been paying attention. I was more focused on starting my plan to walk up to East 14th to take the bus to the library.

I heard her say something about meeting a woman and her daughter. "What did you say, Mama?"

"I knew you weren't paying attention. Sit down." She went on to tell me she had met a woman and her daughter who were both albino. My head shot up, looking at her directly for the first time. Had she said what I thought she'd said?

"You did? What did they look like? Were they pretty?"

I had never met anyone else albino at that point in my life. I couldn't believe it. Why was she so lucky? Why had I not been with her?

"Yes, they were very pretty. That's just it. I met them in the hair color aisle. I was going to get some color for my hair when I saw them. The lady told me that she and her daughter colored their hair and no one knew they were albino." She was beaming with excitement. Her face was all happy and shiny while she talked.

"Wait a minute!" I said. "How could people not know?" My library trip was forgotten, replaced by a dreading in my heart. My stomach suddenly was tight. What was Mama saying, really saying? While I listened, I was trying to figure this all out for myself.

A knot in my stomach told me Mama was up to something, but I didn't know what. Oblivious to my sudden quiet, Mama went on.

"They color their hair, and they wear makeup. They looked normal like everybody else." I said nothing. "So, I got to thinking, well, I had to tell them about you, and we all thought that you could dye your hair too." I'd begun to chew on my nails, which she noticed and made me stop.

"I don't want to dye my hair." I would look strange. I envisioned myself with dark brown or black hair, looking like a freak. Mother went on telling me she thought I would look good with my hair a different color.

"We would be similar, you and I, since I color my hair too." I wasn't convinced. We sat, our knees touching, while she did all she could to convince me about the hair color.

"See . . . look what I bought for you." Mama emptied out the white bags with the Pay 'n Save name on them. There was a box that had Nice 'N Easy printed on it. There was a White lady with yellow blonde hair on the box. "See, it's not dark at all," Mama said convincingly. The box sat in my hand as I gazed down at it. I knew there was no way out of this crazy idea she had. Mama would make it seem like I had a choice when we both knew I didn't.

"And I didn't tell you the best part," she went on. "You can wear makeup."

Did she say makeup? Wait a minute, I told myself. I had been told I would have to wait until high school to wear makeup. And now if I let Mama dye my hair I can wear makeup! I could not believe my ears. "I can wear makeup?" I asked in a small voice. Cradling my face in her hands, Mama told me yes, I could.

I was sent off to gather up some old towels, the comb, and shampoo and conditioner, and to put the kitchen chair near the sink where the light was best. While I did as I had been told, Mama called her mother, inviting everyone over for dinner that night. Minutes later I sat with an old blue towel draped across my shoulders, getting my hair dyed for the first time. I watched Mama mix the dye, which smelled like bleach. She wore clear, plastic gloves. I had shoulder-length hair that was washed weekly, left to dry in the sunlight, and then carefully straightened with the pressing comb, then curled. As she applied the cold, foul-smelling mixture to my hair, I watched small globs of the concoction land on the towel. It looked like poop. I was terrified my hair would come out looking like poop. I did my best to not cry.

Mama talked on the phone the entire time she worked the dye into my hair. I sat with my head lowered, thinking. Makeup. I get to wear makeup. She had shown me the eyebrow pencil and mascara she'd bought. They were the lightest brown she could find. I asked to go to the bathroom before she would rinse the color out of my hair. Closing the door behind me I stood on tiptoe in the mirror. It was bad. Bad as I had thought it would be. My hair did look like poo. Maybe if it looks really bad I won't have to go to school, I told myself. School. Oh, my God, how would I go to school on Monday? The day before I had looked just like me and now . . . now my hair looked like poo. I felt Mama's presence before I saw her. "It won't look like this when I rinse it out, baby."

"Are you sure?" I did not believe her.

Once the dye was washed out, my hair shampooed and conditioned, I toweled it dry. Once again, I found myself in the bathroom mirror. My hair was yellow blonde. It didn't look like the lady's hair on the box. I breathed a sigh of relief.

I sat on the edge of the bathtub blow-drying my hair, so Mama could straighten and curl it. While I dried my hair, I worried what school would be like on Monday. Would people laugh at me, thinking I was pretending to be someone other than who I was? Would I just be ignored like usual? I hoped I would be ignored.

Back in the kitchen chair, my hair was straightened with the hot comb. I hated the hot comb because my ears or neck always got burned and I would be told it was my own fault. Today I managed to escape being burned. As Mama did my hair, she told me how lovely it looked. She told me how smooth and shiny my hair was. I was allowed to run to look in the mirror once more between the pressing and curling. I was amazed. I liked the color, sort of. While I still didn't look like the woman on the box, my hair did look good. Curling my hair took far less time than straightening it did. The black, thin, iron curler sat on the stove just as the straightening comb did, to heat. Mama was putting a loose curl, or bump as we called it, on my hair. She didn't want to put too much stress on my hair, she'd said. When she was done and had styled me to her liking, I was allowed to see the newest version of myself. Wow, did I ever look different. I looked like somebody I might see on the cover of Seventeen, a magazine for teen girls.

We returned to Mama's bedroom where she took the eyebrow pencil, mascara, eye shadow, and blush from their packaging. Carefully, she applied each. Once done, she applied a coat of coral pink lipstick to my lips and stood back to admire her work. Passing me a handheld mirror, she waited for my response. For the first time, I had lips. I had eyes and eyebrows and eyelashes.

I could see my face. I was amazed. This was very cool. Before I couldn't really see my face in detail. I didn't notice the nuances of my facial structure. I knew how my lashes, brows, nose, cheeks, and mouth felt as I touched them, often memorizing it all, but I had never seen myself. Looking up at my mother, I was speechless. Finally, I threw my arms around her, thanking her. I liked what I saw. No longer did I think of myself as a blob like the Pillsbury Dough Boy or like the cartoon ghost, Casper. I thought of myself as a person. I thought of myself as pretty. I stared at my reflection for a long time. I wanted to cry because I was happy, but Mama told me my mascara would run. So instead I traced the parts of my face my fingers knew so well and admired them with newfound eyes.

I began to worry about what Felecia would say. Even though I was older, I always worried about what she would say, for she had always been the pretty girl in our family. She barely noticed. All she cared about was when did she get to wear makeup. Clinton just stared at me, and Greg wasn't home.

Later we all piled in the car to go to our grandparents' house for dinner. It took twenty minutes to drive from Holly Street over to the huge house on 39th Avenue. Sometimes Mama drove through town, taking the scenic route as she called it, which led us from our neighborhood over to MacArthur Boulevard, past Mills College, then onto more of MacArthur to 39th Avenue where we would wind our way up the hill to its crest, turning onto a private drive that held entry to three homes. My grandparents' home was in the middle, cushioned on one side by blackberry bushes that we would pick from every summer. Turning into the large driveway, Mama stopped the car. We all piled out as soon as the engine stopped. The door to the house opened before any of us could knock.

Grandmother was a short, round woman who always had a smile and whose laugh was contagious. Grandmother screamed when she saw me. Her scream startled the three of us kids. She made me turn around and around, taking me in. We gathered at the kitchen table rather than the big dining room table, said grace, and had dinner. The sun was on the other side of the house this time of day, which allowed me to sit facing the large picture window looking out onto the lawn. I could watch the sky change from light blue to a dusky color as the sun made its way west, heading toward the ocean.

I sat at the table with Mother and Grandmother, sensing a difference. I was being treated differently. I knew I wasn't a little girl any longer, but so much of the time I still got treated like I was fragile. Like I could break at any moment. Halfway through dinner, I watched as Grandfather drove up and parked his grey Impala. Felecia and Clint started yelling his name, jumping up from the table to greet him as he entered the house. In the hallway that divided the house, his laughter filled the space. The three of us watched as he hugged and tickled my sister and brother. Reaching into his pocket, a quarter appeared for each of them. Granddaddy was always handing out change when he saw us. He told us everybody needed to keep a little change in their pocket at all times.

Standing in the doorway to the kitchen, he watched us at the table. "Well, who's this movie star sitting at my table?" he bellowed. I sat taller, gently shaking my hair to show off my new look.

"Come give me some sugar," he cooed. I stood, giving him a kiss on the cheek. I was wrapped in a big bear hug, his scruffy face scratching my cheeks. I didn't always want to be hugged by him because he seemed to hug me extra long.

"You look all grown up," he whispered in my ear. "Granddaddy will have something special for you later. Just come see me before you leave." I wriggled free of his hold excusing myself to the bathroom.

"Now, Clint, look what you've gone and done to her. You've upset her," I heard Grandmother say as I left the room. I knew he was pecking her on the cheek by the way Grandmother was laughing.

"Awww, Mama, give Daddy some sugar," I heard him saying. "It won't hurt, I promise." Grandmother pretended to avoid his kisses, even though I knew she liked them. She had told me once that a girl had to play hard to get sometimes, even after she was married. I didn't really understand, so I just nodded when she'd told me. Emerging once again, it was I who stood in the kitchen doorway watching the adults talk. In just a few minutes I had gone from feeling grown up to feeling really awkward, not knowing where I fit.

We all gathered to leave. "Now go tell Granddaddy goodbye," Grandmother reminded us. In their home, he had one room that he mostly spent time in. It was like a little family room that you walked into when you came into the house from the middle door, and most everyone used the middle door. The only exceptions to this were when we had a party there or when Grandmother served as hostess to her church ladies.

The room had a sofa, and a couple of chairs, and a television, along with a stereo. One end of the room housed a small wet bar. It was his space. It was where he could have a drink at the end of the day or play his records. The ones Grandmother referred to as devil music. We kids were welcomed in this room. Here we could relax, free from fear of touching anything that might break. My sister and brother ran ahead of me, offering their goodbyes. By the time I made it to the room, both were spinning on barstools, making themselves dizzy. Standing at the entry that held no door, I called out, "Goodbye, Granddaddy!"

He sat in his recliner, motioning me over to him. Slowly I approached. I stepped to the right side of the chair, offering him a kiss on the cheek. Instead I was swung around easily by him, landing on his lap. I struggled, not wanting to be held. He held tighter. I could smell the whisky on his breath. His attention made my skin crawl. Mother's voice pierced the room as she approached, calling us all to the door. I was let go. I went to move as far away as I could. He held onto the back of my blue jeans and placed a bill in my pocket. I hurried to the door, seeking the safety of the night-lit sky. Alone, I looked up, attempting to find the Big Dipper. Here I could always see the stars. Finding the Big Dipper, I then tried my best to locate its small counterpart. I took huge breaths to clear my head and calm my heart. His last words to me had been whispered quickly. He told me, "Remember that you are my pretty girl, my movie star." All the excitement and pride I'd felt about having my hair dyed and wearing makeup seemed strange and dirty.

In the car, I barely listened to the conversation around me. I gazed out the window, taking in all the lights. I loved the dark. For one, there was no sun. Two, I could see the same places we drove past earlier differently. Coming around the bend onto MacArthur, we drove by Mills College, which was shielded by a sea of trees from onlookers. I imagined this was what a forest looked like. We crossed Seminary Avenue onto Camden. The night was quiet as the car wound its way from the cemetery. We passed by my school, finally ending up on Bancroft. I remembered the money in my pocket. I told myself I would not spend it. It was creepy money. I'd only gotten it because Granddaddy forced me to sit on his lap. We turned on 69th, driving by the house my older brother's girlfriend lived in. We turned left again on Arthur Street to 73rd, where we turned right again. I loved when Mama gave us a maze to go through to get home. We went four more blocks, finally turning onto our street. Our house was third from the corner. In the backseat, Felecia and Clinton slept, oblivious. I had calmed down, shrugging off the exchange with Granddaddy as nothing.

Alone in my room I pulled the money from my back pocket. It was a ten-dollar bill. This was my allowance for the entire month. I took in a breath. I thought about what I might be able to buy with this money and knew even then I would spend it. I knew I would find myself in Pay 'n Save at some point. I could wear makeup. I carefully tucked the money away in my diary, putting the diary beneath my mattress for safekeeping.

In bed that night I thought about everything that had taken place. Today had been a good day. I was happy Mother had met the other two albinos. I wish I had been with her, but that too was alright since now I looked like them. I was just White.

Two days later, I again found myself on Mama's bed, my face being applied with makeup. I'd gone to her the day before worried about how I would put the stuff on myself. We agreed that I would get up early each day to have her put the mascara and eyebrow pencil on until I was ready to do it myself.

From that point on and for many years after, early mornings would be our time. I would come to love this quiet time of day with my mother. My face made up, I rose to finish getting ready for school.

The walk to school was normal. Groups of kids met up as we walked the mile and a half. I had a solid route which held few variations, but this day led me to walk up Arthur Avenue to Havenscourt where I walked past Greater Emmanuel Church of God in Christ Church, which we attended each week. I cut across Bancroft and walked through Lucky's parking lot, where the year before I'd been beaten up by a girl in my class. This put me on Foothill, where I would cross the street one last time and be at school.

While I walked, I worried what people would say when they saw me. Once at school, I made my way to my favorite teacher's portable. Miss Green was the best. She was a great listener, and always willing to make time whenever I needed to talk to someone or to offer practical words of wisdom when I had hurt feelings from being teased. I'd hoped she would be in her room, and she was. I stood a few moments, my eyes adjusting from the bright morning sunlight to the artificially lit room. I waited for her to notice me.

Finally, unable to stand her silence, I said, "Good morning, Miss Green! Notice anything different about me?" I stood, allowing her to take in the new me. Miss Green turned her full attention to me, settling finally on my face. The one and only question she asked was whether or not I liked it. There was no judgment. No "Why would you have done this to yourself?" There was only the gentle smile giving me permission to like or dislike the newly created me. I stand forever in gratitude for that response. She let me go on and on about the entire process until glancing at the clock I was reminded I had a class to attend.

Five minutes later, I found myself sitting in algebra class. This was the class I hated most. The work was easy. Making sense of the numbers was a breeze. The teacher, on the other hand, held a mean, grumpy disposition, likely from teaching for too long. Mrs. Alexander was strict and came off as just plain mean. She

didn't accept excuses. Don't even think about turning in homework late. A collective groan filled the brightly lit classroom the
very first day when

Grump Alexander had slowly and clearly stated her class rules,
expectations, and requirements. Three tardies meant a half a
grade reduction, missed homework could not be replaced, no
matter how you tried to talk her into it. Disrespectful language,
talking in class, or not paying attention would get you in the
best case an essay to write, even though this was algebra. In the
worst case, such behavior earned a walk to the vice principal's
office. She was hard. And yet you knew where you stood at all
times with her.

Only once was I the focus of her displeasure. We were doing
the math section of the yearly standardized tests, and I wrote
my responses on a blank sheet of paper instead of filling in the
bubbles with the requisite number 2 pencil. Handing in the
papers, I was met with a hostile stare, whereupon I was told
to fill in the bubbles or else. From the inception of the CTBS
tests, I had been told to fill in my responses on a separate sheet
of paper and my VH teacher (visually handicapped) would fill
in the tiny bubbles for me. I was given this accommodation
because I was unable to see well enough to complete the test
properly. Until junior high school when the test was admin-
istered, I had been read the questions and possible answers
and made my selections orally with Mrs. Finnafoss filling in
the bubbles. Now in 8th grade, I was required to take the test
with my peers. Explaining to Mrs. Alexander what needed to

happen was pointless. I knew she would not accept my word for it. I left the test paper, my name written neatly at the top of the page on her desk.

To my horror, three weeks later I got my report card and saw a C marked as the grade in algebra when I knew I had earned an A. Distressed, I showed my parents, who decided to confront this teacher at the school open house. I stood off to the side of the room, simultaneously embarrassed and vindicated, while my towering father leaned over to discuss the reported grade with Mrs. Alexander. I watched as she brought out the Scantron sheet used for the CTBS test for his perusal. Mother stood next to him, looking as well. Once they saw the sheet filled with small, empty bubbles, my father's easy manner altered. Never raising his voice, he stood to his full 6'3" height, which was intimidating. It was explained once again about my vision challenges and what arrangements had been made.

The formidable algebra teacher cringed, realizing her mistake. She began to backpedal her words, catching as she sought to explain herself. Mother was far less polite. She let the uncomfortable teacher know that no one should be punished for what they could not truly do. Mrs. Alexander was told that she had until the next afternoon to change the grade to what it should be, which was determined to be an A according to the grade book. A part of me felt for the algebra teacher because I knew all too well what dealing with my parents was like. I also knew that she hated me and that I would really have to work hard for the rest of the year to stay clear of her wrath.

So that Monday, my hair colored light ash blonde, my face made up, I did all I could to draw as little attention to myself as possible. Pretending to not hear the whispers around me, I focused on my math book. When the final bell rang, everyone looked directly at Mrs. Alexander. A few whispers lingered behind me. Two girls were talking about me. All of a sudden, my confidence about my new self dissipated. I felt exposed and uncomfortable. My cheeks burned with embarrassment. The girls were called out and told to walk to the front of the room to face the strictest teacher in the school. Lowering my head, I peeked to my left, noticing others doing the same thing. Some stifled snickers with coughs, while others did what they could to stay under the radar. Strands of golden blonde hair touched my arm. For better or worse, this was my hair, I told myself, so I might as well make it for better. Hearing the door close I sat up looking for the two chastised students. They were gone. And so went my first day at school as a blonde. There was no discussion about what had just happened. Class proceeded as usual.

Life in the halls between classes was a completely different story. Everybody noticed me. A few girls said they liked the blonde. They told me the color brought out my face. Still others told me they were jealous that I could wear makeup. When I shared that it had been my mom's idea, that alone made me suddenly cool. Smiling, I closed the locker door. The two girls from algebra stood behind me. "You look stupid," one said. "Don't think that makes you normal. You'll always be a freak," said the other. My face crumpled, cheeks burning with hurt and shame. Holding in the tears that stung my eyes wanting to spill forward, I walked away quickly, hurrying upstairs to my next class. "So much for looking normal," I muttered to myself. I would never fit in, and I knew it.

Fitting in is all I ever wanted as a teenager. This is what all teenagers aspire toward. When you look different, act different, think different, are different from everybody else, you stand out. Standing out puts you at risk for being the target of unwanted attention. You risk being an individual with your own thoughts. You risk being included and accepted for who you are. I wish I had known these things when I was young. I wish all teenagers, all children, know this, and I wish the world were kinder. Thankfully I am no longer so naive as to believe we all get treated equally, for this is not so. As a girl who didn't see well and as a girl with white skin in a community of brown, I was other.

In my neighborhood, where I had cousins who lived at the end of the block and cousins who lived around the corner, I was liked, I had friends, and I was looked after by lots of the mothers as though I was one of their own. If someone saw me walking up the street with my arm raised to my forehead trying to block out the sun, she would call out, asking me where my sunglasses were and why wasn't I wearing them. If it was a warm day, I'd be told I should be wearing long sleeves and for god's sake where was my hat and don't make them call my mamma. In my neighborhood, this was love. This attention was care because no one wanted to hear about me, or any child for that matter, being in distress. On my block, I was safe. Back then, everyone looked out for everyone else's children. It was just the way things were done.

OPEN SEASON

The year I turned fifteen my life became unbearable. I know most fifteen-year-old girls believe life is unbearable. Mine truly was. That summer rarely was I able to avoid my grandfather. Stuck at home looking after my sister and brother, I was easily accessible to him. He would come over to the house or call, summoning me to the bar around the corner from where we lived. The bar was a long, narrow building half a block from our house, sandwiched between two other buildings, one of which was an apartment building where some of our cousins lived.

I knew not to make Grandfather wait too long because he would grow angry if he had to wait. The pretense would be for me to count inventory in the back room. I never counted anything other than time before he would be done molesting me. With each slap of skin against skin, each in and out, tears fell, leaving splotches on the unopened boxes. He always left the storeroom first, making it seem like he was just giving me instructions before reentering the bar. His patrons knew what he was up to.

The storeroom was where he took women. Barely large enough to hold three people, the room filled with boxes and a stool or a folding chair or two was lit by one hanging light. When I was in there with him, Grandfather would offer all kinds of sweet talk, calling me his special girl. I never wanted to believe him, and yet at times I actually did. I wanted—no, needed—to be special. I was far from special anywhere. I was an outcast, teased mercilessly from the time I began school because of my appearance. I was a fair-skinned, white-haired, pink-eyed monstrosity, someone once told me. I had been only ten and didn't know what a monstrosity was and so found my way to a dictionary. My cheeks burned from the hurt. I didn't tell my mother.

Not telling my mother was something that became a habit. I lived under threat of being beaten or killed if I told her or anyone what Grandfather was doing to me. I believed his threats because I knew he was capable of making them a reality.

My best friend went with me to Planned Parenthood where I learned I was pregnant. With my face tear-streaked, sitting numb on the hard, plastic chair, I listened as I was given my options from the nurse practitioner. To Wanda's credit, she just held my hand while I cried. Neither of us knew what to do. I knew I would have to tell my mother. She paid attention to when my sister and I got our periods. I guess this is how she kept tabs on us. Guilt-ridden, I slept little, trying to figure my way out of being pregnant. I knew Mama had been pregnant at fifteen. I knew this because I could do the math. I wrote her a letter, telling her I was like her, just like her.

I placed the letter on her dresser. Letter in hand, she shook with rage, confronting me. Telling me I had planned this and that I was in fact not like her. I was supposed to be smart. And, if I was so goddamned smart, why did I let this happen. Saying nothing, which was safest in that moment, I blushed with shame. Later that day, I stood before both of my parents, she the inquisitioner and my father her silent sentry. Refusing to answer their question about which boy had done this only fueled Mama's anger. Shaking, I stood silent, though in my head I was screaming, "Your good-for-nothing daddy did this to me, and you know it!" I was well practiced in listening to Mama and also thinking of other things simultaneously.

It was a surprise to all of us when I spoke those words aloud. An eerie silence filled the room. It felt like I was underwater, and all was muffled around me. It was only when I lay on the floor I realized she'd slapped me and called me a liar. Saying that her father would do no such thing. What I learned from this was telling the truth made no difference. I walked away from that room knowing my life was only going to get worse.

When news of my pregnancy became public, it was akin to the commencing of hunting season. Those with and without permits had free license. I was attacked from all sides. Each word and action wounded me. Mother was furious, raging at me about how I could be so stupid. She referred to me in the third person, remarking how her/my intellect had failed her/me in this one important area.

One Saturday evening, two weeks before an abortion, I was made to stand in front of the wall heater in the dining room while my sister and two cousins sat at the oval oak table. Disgraced, I was the example used to demonstrate to the others the folly of spreading one's legs for a boy. Inside part of my spirit was dying.

"It wasn't a boy!" I wanted to shout. "It was your father!" Yet I said nothing. Instead, like the others, I remained silent while Mother and her chosen sister discussed the inconvenience of my condition.

"Are you going to let her keep it?"

"Oh, god no! The procedure is already scheduled. I just have to keep it from Mother."

My cheeks burned with shame and embarrassment. I had not been irresponsible. I had been molested. I had been used by someone I was supposed to trust. I ceased listening and began making a mental list of my favorite books. Little House on the Prairie, Little Women, A Tale of Two Cities, I Know Why the Caged Bird Sings, The Bluest Eye. I took two steps away from the heater. It was on, and the heat was unbearable. Mother glared at me. I was in a cage without bars. I was acutely aware that my movements were restricted.

"If she'd really been smart, she would have at least pretended to have a period. Spread ketchup on the pad or something. Goes to show you that book smart isn't everything." They both laughed as my aunt mocked me.

I held my hands at my sides in fists. Her words stung. I was proud of my intellect. I performed well in school. School was my escape. Their verbal assault continued until they grew bored. We were dismissed. I had told the truth but hadn't been believed. We sat in the kitchen, saying nothing to one another. I had no idea each of us bore his scars.

My grandfather no longer had to worry about allowing for my period. No matter how I timed my arrival home after school, he found me. If I got off the bus at a different stop, the one that was after the bar, I'd see him standing outside. Even if I managed to avoid him, he had the uncanny ability of knowing when I would be home alone. Every part of me would tighten whenever I heard his heavy footsteps or his authoritative and somehow cheerful voice as he entered our home. Like a docile pet, I was led to a bed. I once bit the back of my hand so hard I drew blood. Sometimes it was as though I watched what was happening to me. I was not that girl in pain. Other times, I focused on anything other than being molested. I wrote essays in my head, considered the French test I had the next day. I was not in my body.

I don't know how my older brother and his cohorts found out about the pregnancy, but for them I was easy prey, forbidden yet already damaged. I was home from school making dinner. This was often my job. I'd cut a whole chicken as I had been taught. Leg and thigh first, then wings were cut from the carcass. Last, I'd separate the breast from the back, cutting each into smaller pieces. I did this almost entirely by feel. I was in the middle of seasoning and flouring the meat when my brother and his buddies came into the kitchen. I said hello and kept to my task.

I felt someone approach me before I saw him. Usually I was off limits because I was my brother's awkward sister. But not today. The tall, lanky, dark boy put his arms around me. At first, I went rigid. I knew what this meant. I pushed his hands away from my waist. He persisted. Another hand covered my mouth, so no one would hear me scream. My legs gave out as tears streamed down my face. I wrapped my arms around myself, crossed my legs, and tried to twist away, but there were too many of them. One by one they took their turn. They were sweaty, each desperate to mark territory. The greatest humiliation wasn't that my brother, who had been my protector, had allowed his friends to rape me, but that he too participated. I was left on the floor like a discarded rag.

I thought about The Scarlet Letter. I was no adulteress, but I knew I was tainted. Everyone in my world knew I was tainted. Get up, I told myself. I couldn't. Get up! There was a mess between my legs. I didn't even know where my pants were. If I stay here, I will get in trouble if Mama finds me. At no point did I believe she, my mother, would or could find me and come to my defense. I rolled onto my right side and saw the stove. I was supposed to be frying chicken.

When I stood, I thought I would fall again. The yellow room was too bright, and I was too weak. I walked around the puddle in the middle of the floor and went to clean myself up. Afterward I mopped the floor, opened the back door to air the kitchen, then proceeded to make dinner. I tried not to think about what happened because if I did I would cry.

We always ate dinner together. I was noticeably quiet as was my older brother. I moved food around my plate. I wasn't hungry. Yet I knew I had to eat. We were not allowed to waste food. Each forkful of chicken, peas, and rice lodged in my throat, forcing me to swallow or choke. I looked at no one, just my plate.

I tuned the conversations out. All I could think about was how could he let his friends do that to me? I chanced looking at him. The look I was given dared me to say something, knowing already that I wouldn't. I stared back at my plate, which collected the first tear and the second and the third before I asked to be excused from the table. Mama demanded I tell her what was wrong with me. I couldn't talk. I hugged myself, arms crushing my swollen breasts. I ached everywhere. My tears flowed freely. "I have a headache. It was bright today." It was a lie, but it was the best I could do. I was dismissed.

I lay on my bed in the dark listening. I hated the family I was born into. I hated being me.

I used to hate November and Thanksgiving in particular. Both were acute reminders of having been molested and aborting the only child I would ever carry.

The day after Thanksgiving in 1977 I woke early. Unable to eat, I dressed and joined Mama in the car. I stared out the window, half listening as she berated me for upsetting her life. I knew this was a one-sided conversation. No, I wouldn't tell my grandmother. No, it wouldn't happen again. No, I wouldn't tell her who was responsible.

When she parked, the silence was unbearable.

"Look at me!" Mama yelled, making me jump. "Look at me, dammit!"

Our eyes met, mine filled with hurt, shame, and with tears that with one blink cascaded lava hot, burning my cheeks. Hers filled with anger and sadness. She had known all along. Yet she'd done nothing.

We retraced the same path we'd covered the day before. I'd been there for a pre-op examination. The doctor was brusque with me, criticizing me for flinching at his touch while he inserted a Laminaria. "If you could open your legs to get pregnant, you can open them for this too." His harsh, judgmental words made me feel even smaller, more wounded. I longed for the sunglasses I'd left at home to buffer me from the brightly lit corridor as well as the scorn-filled eyes of the doctor.

My mother did not stay with me after checking me in for outpatient surgery. She did not hold my hand. She did not comfort me. She was gone, absent while the surgeon removed my unborn child.

I became ill on the way home, the aftereffect of the anesthesia. Mama pulled over, stroking my back as I retched. Part of me didn't want her comfort, but a greater part needed her to love me. Once home, sweaty and wracked with pain, I took refuge in my bed, curled up as I imagined my baby had been.

I did not really want to have a baby, let alone my grandfather's. Yet I believed that perhaps this child might have resembled me, might have had albinism. I would never know because the decision was made for me, without my input. Now, decades later, I am grateful for the abortion. I know life would have been much more challenging. Also, if that child had been born female, she too would have been at risk. And equipped with the knowledge I have now, I cannot say who would have survived.

After the abortion, I closed in on myself, shutting the world out as much as I could. I didn't understand how or why it was that I was being punished for something that wasn't my fault. I was afraid all the time. It wasn't until a couple of months after the abortion when Mother would nearly kill me herself.

My older brother and I had bedrooms downstairs, which we were told over and over again was a privilege. I'd changed the sheets on my bed as I'd been told to do. Mama had come to inspect the downstairs and went crazy. She took one look at the sheets and began yelling at me that they were the wrong ones. Why was I using her sheets? My apologies went unheard. Her arm tightened around my neck as she proceeded to beat me with an extension cord. I pleaded with her to stop, finally just crying as I attempted to defend myself. All I could hear was Mama yelling and the sound of the cord hitting my skin. I think it was the sight of bloody welts that finally made her stop. She threw the cord down, leaving me curled up on the floor where I fell asleep.

I woke to my thirteen-year-old sister whispering softly to me to get up. Together we cleaned the wounds on my arms, legs, and back. The alcohol stung each time she found a new place to disinfect. I bore this pain silently. This pain paled in contrast to what Mama had done to me. I knew she was aware about Grandfather, which made her treatment of me worse. Barely able to walk, I made my way to bed.

The next day was a school day. I was told to wear a turtleneck and not to say anything to anyone about the beating. I rarely spoke to anybody at school anyhow. Who would I tell? I had no friends. Dressed in the softest clothes I could find, my body stiff and sore, I went off to school.

I shuffled from class to class like a zombie saying nothing. Gently I'd ease myself onto the wooden desk seats, trying not to wince in pain. Midday I was called out of class, summoned into the nurse's office. I thought the nurse had somehow learned about the abortion, and I was embarrassed. When I was ushered into her inner office and she shut the door, I was terrified. I was asked if I was okay. A few teachers had noticed I wasn't quite myself. She touched my back, and I cried out. Slowly my turtleneck was raised, revealing oozing welts.

"Please, don't call my mother. She will be so angry. I will get in more trouble. Please, I'll participate more in class. My mother will . . . she will . . . I don't know what she will do, but it won't be good."

This nurse did not know my mother. Mama had told me not to say anything. Yet again, I had no control over what was happening to me. And just like that I was taken to the hospital. The authorities from child protective services were called in, and I watched my mother talk herself out of being cited for abusing me. She and a social worker sat chatting in our living room. I had been called before them, asked how things were, how I was doing. I lied, telling her I was fine. I had been told to say this. I watched as the two women conversed like old friends. The case was dismissed.

On one level, I thought that maybe the social workers would see through Mama. That they would see what else was happening to me. This did not happen, and so Grandfather continued molesting me. The only difference was he would ask me when my period was due. He wasn't taking any chances with getting me pregnant again he'd said. This was my life until I left home.

I poured myself into school. I knew my brain was my way out of Oakland, and I intended to leave. The spring before graduation I learned I'd been accepted into every university I had applied to. This news served as a huge boost in my confidence. And while I wasn't ready to move across the country, I was more than prepared to move to a different part of the state.

GRANDDADDY

I remember when I was little how hearing your voice made me laugh. You would show up at our house, usually unannounced, filling the living room with the rich, scratchy voice that made us kids happy. I would run over to you eagerly whenever you'd call out, "Come sit on Granddaddy's lap!" Like it was the best and safest place to be. I'd nestle into the crook of your arm, giggling when you'd offer up your scratchy cheek for some sugar.

My child-self was oblivious to the distance Mama would place between you and her. Her arms crossed in front of her, folded in a "Let's see what this is all about" stance. She watched rapt, while we children hung on your every word.

I once asked Mama why she was distant toward you. "I used to love him in the way that kids love their daddy as their protector, like when I was five maybe six. I was always happy to see Daddy when he came in at the end of the day. I met him at the door as soon as I heard his voice. Daddy would spin me round and round only to catch me up in his arms when I got dizzy."

You'd always ask the same question. "Now what have you all been doing?" You'd regard us intently as Felecia and I perched on a knee. There was no room left for Greg, so he stood before you. We were secure in the certainty of being loved. You were partial to me even then. An extra hug offered or kiss sought, prolonging an intimacy.

I remember learning to hate you. I learned this hate each time you asserted yourself over me. Each time you opened your pants. I learned to hate my body for reacting to you when all my brain could think was how wrong the act was. I remember how I learned to hate my body for its color. I thought that if I had been brown like everyone else you'd have no interest in me. How wrong I was. I hated my body for responding to your touch. I hated the pleasure I experienced. I did not understand my body was simply doing what bodies do. I blamed myself. There were times I would stand in the shower letting the hot water turn my skin pink. I used to think if I washed myself of you, that if I was cleansed, the incest wasn't as bad. Ha, I was but a child.

Then there were the times I felt special. Those times I was more willing, more compliant because our togetherness made you so very happy. When you were happy, you didn't scare me or the other kids. And being the oldest girl, I wanted my sister and younger brother to be unafraid. I liked protecting them from you.

You know I used to hate November. Grandmother headed to Memphis every year at that time. I was in high school and was required to stay at your house to cook for the people as we called them. The board and care patients who lived downstairs. I didn't like those men either. We knew their presence brought money into the house, and that without a place to live those men would be lost, Grandmother's words. So, we did our best to ignore them. However, when Grandmother was away I had to deal with them. It was my job to cook for them, breakfast, and dinner. Sandwiches would be left for lunch. I don't know how you convinced Mama to let me stay, but you did. Those times I hated most.

I would get Clinton ready for school every morning, make breakfast for everyone, and still manage to get myself to school on time, an hour from your house. You would come in late from the bar. I would lie in bed terrified you would come for me. I would pray you wouldn't. Rarely were those prayers answered. If I resisted, too often you grew angry and violent, dragging me from my bed to yours. I was a thing to be used, to provide satisfaction to you. Afterward I'd be sent back to bed with a warning not to tell anyone or else I knew what would happen.

Do you know what it is to live in fear, all the time, every day, every moment? Of course, you don't, because you were never a victim. This is what you did to me, caused me to fear everyone and everything. I was terrified of my own shadow, afraid you would be there when I turned around.

The young men in the family watched you. You were their model for getting girls. And because they saw how you treated me, how you took from me, some of them did the same. My body was theirs to explore and experiment on, preparing them for future girlfriends. I used to think you had told them to do this. I used to believe that we had no choice, following your orders. How fucking dare you and them!

CHAMPIONS

Throughout my life there have been those who watched over me, looked out for me, mentored me, protected me, and stood up for me. As a young child, I had no idea what this really meant. However, as an adult, I am acutely aware that I have become who I am in part because of the people who held these roles in my life.

My mother will always be my champion. My birth was a source of shame. She was but a girl herself. She had been molested and impregnated by her father, my father. And then there was the unexpected surprise of a White baby. She managed to overcome the stigma and fight on my behalf. She and her husband demanded I be allowed into public school long before access to education for students with disabilities was a requirement. They taught me how to self-advocate from a young age, throughout my years of education, for which I am deeply indebted.

There was the yard teacher in elementary school who brought a bag of Little Golden Books monthly for me to read as I sat in the shade during recess. She was also responsible in quietly encouraging other children to include me in four-square, a popular ball game, which is still played in many schools worldwide. Of course, I had to stay in the shade. Somehow the kids knew this without me telling them.

There were the three different specialists, teachers of the visually handicapped, as was their title back then. Mrs. Finnefoss, or Mrs. F, and Miss Croda were instrumental in my adjusting to school. Massive math books and readers magically appeared in the classroom each year. The books were so large they took up an entire table. Initially I was uncertain about these women. At five, the only White people I knew were doctors. In time, however, I grew to cherish the hour out of the classroom daily with them. With them I learned to type on a manual Remington typewriter. I read aloud. I completed math assignments. I thrived. In junior high school, I met Mrs. Ramage. She was different from Mrs. F. She further taught me the value of self-advocacy. After the first year of junior high, she didn't meet with teachers on my behalf. I was required to do this for myself. I discovered later that she would follow up with the teachers to ensure I had done my part. She gave me the push and the opportunity to learn a valuable skill—the ability to take charge. By high school, I was requesting the books on tape I needed and the textbooks for all my classes. Mrs. Ramage prepared me for college, for life.

There are many teachers who impacted my life in a positive manner. From Mrs. Mace, my second grade teacher who recognized my love of books and nurtured that love, to Mrs. Grant, my sixth grade teacher who suggested I be tested for the Gifted and Talented Education (GATE) program. My first French teacher, Madame Warner, from whom I developed a passion of the culture and language. Mr. Ferrero, my high school Social Studies teacher who believed in an A/F grading system, was equal parts friendly and amusing. He often stood at the door greeting students, helping himself to proffered French fries purchased during the break. Double jointed, he was a contortionist, often twisting his tall, lean frame into a pretzel while sitting at his desk. We thrived in his classroom, learning history and the importance of human connection.

The two teachers who are truly noteworthy continue to be part of my life today. Both extraordinary women, Mattie Green Johnson and Carol Olney Dean, deserve special recognition.

I began at Frick Junior High in the fall of 1974. I was shy. I knew no one, and I visibly differed from everyone else in the entire school. My class schedule indicated that my English class was out in a portable classroom. I hated finding new places. I still do. I exited the main building, located the group of portables I needed, and made my way to the final one in the row. The day was hot, and I raised my arm to block the sun. Walking down the path, I noticed the buildings were here buffered from the sun's harsh rays. Maybe this won't be so bad, I told myself.

In elementary school, my third and fourth grade classes had been in portables too. But there had been no protection from the sun. They were out in the open. I welcomed this respite. The numbers were big, which I liked. I stepped into English class. I sighed with relief because the room was cool and dim. As my eyes adjusted, I was greeted with a warm hello. Of course she knew who I was. I listened for the direction of her voice as I tentatively walked further into the room. I closed and re-opened my eyes. Before me stood a woman shorter than me. She had a short Afro and a vibrant smile. "Hello, Ma'am." I felt really awkward because I didn't know what else to say.

"You may sit wherever you like."

"Thank you," I offered. My head was spinning. I had never been given this option. I always sat in the front row. And now I didn't have to. My joy quickly shifted to unease as I realized I wouldn't be able to see the chalkboard if I sat in any other row. The almost always present knot in my stomach gnawed at me.

"It's okay," she said. "It is really alright. I know. I will always have written notes for you." My head shot up. I didn't even know I was holding it down.

"Really?" Surprise and hope pushed the knot away. I quickly found a seat three rows from the front of the room. This act of kindness and compassion were but the first of countless acts on Mattie Green's part.

One afternoon, Miss Green (I never called her by her first name) drove me to my grandparents' home. She was aware of the abuse, and frankly she had had enough of it. She'd witnessed my despondency. She'd seen my transformation from an engaged student to a skittish, terrified girl. Miss Green, now Mrs. Johnson, was and continues to be a woman of God. It was her faith and foundation that allowed her that day to do something no one in my life had ever considered.

She held my hand as we walked from the car to the front door to their house. When Grandfather opened the door, he was surprised to see us. He stood to the side to allow me entrance. Yet I did not move. Ms. Green never let go of my hand. In confronting him, she rebuked Satan and cast a light of God's protection around me. There was a lot of yelling. What impacted me most, causing me to shrink behind Miss Green, was Grandfather threatening my favorite teacher and confidant. If she was afraid, there were no visual signs. She held steadfast to her purpose. Terrified, I stood by two of the most powerful people in my life, shaking. One who loved me and was willing to risk everything for my well-being, and one who claimed love, but held ownership through twisted relation.

Although my circumstances did not change that day or for the remainder of my adolescence, what remains for me is the willingness and fierce tenacity this petite woman possessed and the strength of her conviction for calling out deceit, harm, and abuse.

Miss Green, or Mother Mattie as I now refer to her, continued to provide respite well into my mid-twenties. Her guidance and acceptance served me well. I gained confidence, maintained boundaries with my family of origin, and emerged from my protective shell.

When I think about mothering, I often think of how I was parented and how I wish I had been. I reflect on the two women who shaped me. The two women I call Mom.

When I began high school, I had a difficult time adjusting. There were three buildings, each of which had two floors. There was no O and M (Orientation and Mobility) like there is now for visually impaired students. I had to learn where I needed to be by squinting, counting doors, and praying. No one—not me or Mrs. Ramage or my parents—informed the teachers about my vision challenges. This led to me failing algebra. I was devastated. I had never received anything lower than a C, and a C was rare. So when I saw an F on my report card, I was terrified. I failed because I couldn't see the blackboard and using graph paper was visually beyond my ability. So, being the overachiever I was and still am, I returned that fall and took the same class with the same teacher to prove to her I could do the work. This determination on my part led to Carol Olney taking an interest in me. She took me under her wing. "I could tell you were troubled," Carol told me years later. "So I did what I could, which was to make sure you had what you needed academically."

Carol did that and more. Some Fridays my best friend and I would climb into Carol's car and head off to her neighborhood, the White part of Oakland, to do errands and to visit Fentons on Piedmont Avenue for ice cream. These excursions were pure joy. I was acutely aware of being stared at especially whenever we went to Piedmont Market. We were a unique trio—a tall, curvy, White woman, a Black girl, and me, who people could not figure out. One smile from Mom held a multitude of emotions. I dare you to say something. Anything. "Yes, these are my girls." And, "Don't even try me," were but a few. I recognized these expressions and understood that with her they meant I was safe.

Our friendship continued after I completed high school. When I was home on a break from college the spring of my freshman year, my mother, who had always encouraged the friendship with Carol, conveyed to me that I might as well call her Mom as well, since she was just as much my mom as she was. I was flabbergasted. Mother was having her own struggles with depression, and later she would struggle with drugs. This was her way of making sure I was taken care of. She recognized I needed additional nurturing and mothering. We both knew she was unable to provide me with it. My mother's willingness to share me with Carol was a gift to us all.

BREAKING SILENCE

I originally wrote this as a journal entry in 1985 after meeting with my grandparents. I was twenty-three.

Today I decided I would no longer be silent.

"Your silence will no longer protect you," my inner voice said as I dressed for the day's activities. "Dress protectively," whispered the voice. I selected my deep teal corduroy skirt and the rose silk blouse I often paired with it.

The day was perfect, a cold rainy Friday in November. November, always a month of change in my life. No longer will I lie to protect others, I told myself as I set off for the meeting. Halfway to the restaurant, anxiety overcame me in something like an ocean wave crashing against the shore. I persevered. My grandparents were already seated when I entered the restaurant, both visibly uncomfortable. Was this the first time they'd been somewhere together since the separation? It had taken great engineering to convince them to come. "Your silence will not protect you," came the comforting mantra from my inner voice. Breathing deeply, I approached the table. Had they arrived together? Likely not, since they disliked one another. She was wearing a simple, though assuredly expensive, beige dress, and he wore one of the many suits she purchased for him while they'd been married.

We sat, me across from the two of them, discussing trivial things—weather, our jobs, me studies in school. Quickly, safe topics evaporated, leaving an awkward silence in its wake. "I imagine you're wondering why I asked that you meet with me today?" They nodded. "I've decided the time has come for me to no longer hide and remain silent." For a moment I was exhilarated. The tables had turned. I waited.

"What do you mean hide and be silent?" Grandmother asked.

"I woke up last week realizing I've been silent my entire life."

"But you've always talked a lot, ever since you were a baby," Grandfather said.

I refrained from rolling my eyes. Was he serious?

"Grandfather, I don't mean in the literal sense. I mean I've endured too much pain in silence." They stared at each other as if to ask, is our granddaughter crazy? I pressed on. Stomach in knots, I swallowed, forcing lunch to remain where it was. "I brought you here to discuss our family secret, incest." How I remained upright I do not know, but I did in spite of the vertigo. Or was it terror?

The silence was heavy as we avoided looking at one another. Mustering courage, I gazed intently at them, forcing myself to focus. Grandfather's eyes were cold with anger, his face set with hardened lines. Once I'd been terrified of threats he'd used to overpower me, but no more. Grandmother stilled, her face red with fury. Only her lips moved as she prayed to herself. I wondered if she would believe me.

"When I was a teenager, your husband raped me repeatedly for four years. In your house, in my mother's house, on the way to visit my aunts in Oregon, and each time you went to Memphis for the church convention." I was cold and sweaty, hot and damp all at once. I glanced from one to the other, awaiting a response, an answer. There was none. Seconds turned to moments to minutes without one word said.

"Why didn't you tell me?" Grandmother gripped her hands, her knuckles nearly white.

"I tried, but you wouldn't listen, didn't want to, refused to. Somehow you believed God would make it alright. Well, he didn't. In the years since I've left home, I've ceased going to church. I've turned my back on a god who failed me."

Grandfather remained quiet. Maybe that's how it should be, I thought, but I'd expected something. Yet as I watched him, he returned my gaze with those cold, hard, piercing eyes.

My hands were clenched into fists, heart pounding. I was sweating. The silk blouse clung to my clammy skin. Maybe I made a mistake in coming here. I was terrified.

"But, but that was years ago," she said. "You seem okay now."

"Well, I'm not!" I yelled. My fist slammed against the table. "I am ashamed because of what HE did to me. I feel guilty because . . . well, I ask myself if it was my fault even though I understand it wasn't." I glared at my grandfather. He'd begun to fidget, shifting his weight in the chair.

"But you—" She stopped talking, seeing the hurt and betrayal in my eyes.

She stared at the man who had once been her husband. He sat, head lowered, unable to meet her gaze. "Have you nothing to say about this?" Her voice shook. "Have you?"

"I, I didn't do anything wrong," he stammered.

"Nothing wrong? Are you kidding me?" I glanced at people at surrounding tables. Meals forgotten, many sat staring back at me, curious. I did not care what these strangers thought of me. Composure gone, I was unraveling.

"How can you say that Clint?"

I too wanted to know how he could justify molesting me.

"It was my right to teach her about sex," he muttered. "Better me than some boy knocking her up."

Your silence will not protect you.

I was the ball of yarn being kicked about, fraying along the way. Except it was my heart and spirit breaking into small pieces. I struggled to breathe. I recoiled inside. The air filled with the sound of forks coming to a halt. Breaths held in anticipation of further revelation.

"Did it ever occur to you that I didn't want to be taught about sex by you? Did you ever stop to think you were doing something wrong? Did you ever think?" I realized I was yelling then. I felt grandmother's hand touch my own. But I refused to be quieted. "Tell me, what did you think each time you molested me, each time you raped me?" I stood, shaking, trembling with rage.

"Please, dear, please, please lower your voice," Grandmother pleaded. "This is family business."

I lowered myself into the chair, acutely aware that all eyes were upon me. The waiter approached us, nearly sprinting. As he placed the check upon the table, I requested coffee. His disappointment evident, he refilled my cup.

"I only did it because I loved you," Grandfather said after the waiter had gone.

"Love!? Well, I guess you too called it love, Granny, because each time you left town you made me stay with this, this, bastard."

Her concern immediately turned to horror.

"Now leave your grandmother out of this. She had no way of knowing what was happening."

"I strongly disagree." Turning to Grandmother, I continued. "And I think you didn't want to admit the kind of person you married. It was easier. Less guilt for you."

"Now I said leave your grandmother out of this. It doesn't concern her." There was an edge of threat to his voice.

"So now you're going to protect her?" I said skeptically. "No one bothered to protect me." I was shaking so hard I couldn't feel my feet. "And, Grandfather, your voice no longer intimidates me. So don't talk to me about protecting people."

There was no point in addressing this any further. They were complicit in denial. Neither would admit to wrongdoing. Silently I gathered my things. I was calm, amazingly calm as I walked into the rain.

I moved quickly, placing as much distance from the restaurant as I could. Adrenaline fueled my pace. As I approached the Bart station, I doubled over. Sobs poured out as hot tears cascaded down my cheeks. Had I truly believed the outcome would be any different? I was devastated. And yet I had spoken the truth.

PARALLEL LIVES

Our lives have always been parallel. There are differences, but not many. I would say the first of which is how we were each created. You were created out of new love. Your parents were young, married, and strong in who they were. Upon your birth you were celebrated, welcomed into your family. Showered with love and affection, you thrived and were adored by all. You were allowed as a little girl to be fully expressed, a new millennium term meaning you were allowed to be funny, creative, full of life.

Your parents were eighteen and twenty when you were born. They knew love and knew family and knew hard work. Your mother, a petite, dimpled, smiling beauty had captivated your father. He, a young, strong, tall, light-brown-skinned man had been taken in by her the moment he met her and her twin sister. While her sister, Precious, had wanted Clint, it was Laura who won out in the end.

The wedding had been a simple affair. She wore a simple white dress, he a new pair of trousers and white button-down shirt. Though his shoes were worn, they were polished and had been fitted with new laces. Once the wedding and celebrations were over, the new couple left Texas and moved to Bradley, Arkansas, where Clint's family lived. Though Laura had never been far from her own family, she was an adventurer. Living in Bradley was a challenge for Laura. Her new husband was always working, providing for the two of them and his family. He and his brother Jim consistently seemed to have a scheme going on, buying a cow from a White farmer just to take it to the next town to sell it to someone else for a profit. The brothers were rarely parted.

His was a tall family, even the girls managed to be taller than the new bride. This was no issue for Laura as she was accustomed to people being taller than she was. At barely five feet, her happy, no-nonsense nature made up for her size. Everyone generally forgot she was short. Clint's sisters—Lovie, Geneva, Jessie Mae, Verda, Rose Lee, and Willamae—all welcomed and loved their new sister, which was how they regarded her. Laura was grateful for their kindness as she was used to being in a large family.

So when you were born nearly two years after the marriage ceremony, everyone was overjoyed. You were named for the sister who hadn't lived to adulthood. You were fat and healthy, possessed rosy cheeks and a pleasant disposition. It was a sad day for everyone when the three of you left the familiarity and safety of Bradley to drive across country to a state no one knew much about. Oregon.

In truth, though, part of the reason your parents headed west was because your father had been caught sleeping with a White woman. All the running around he did with brother Jim included romancing his way into the beds of women, both Black and White. The story was relayed to me by our northwest cousin. Evidently, Clint had been calling on this one woman a few times a week, always after her husband had gone off to work. The man knew something was going on. One morning he returned home to discover his wife having relations with a colored man. In a rage, the White man told your father that he better not see him around town, otherwise there would be trouble. Translation, he would make sure that particular colored man would be dead. The family gathered up food and what money there was to be had, and within a day the three of you were on your way. Can you imagine how your mother must have felt? Was she shocked at the sudden need to migrate west? Did he present the plan seeking her input, or did he simply announce you were leaving? Likely the latter.

Once in Eugene, the family settled in Tent City along the Willamette River outside city limits. There were no tents, but wooden shanties built by each family. Clint worked on the railroad. Unhappy with living along the river, Clint sent you both to California to join your mother's family. He promised to build you a house and write when it was ready. He insisted. Laura was unsure whether or not she should leave her husband so soon after arriving in this strange state and town where there were few people who were colored. Yet she was secretly overjoyed to get the chance to see her family again. Laura especially missed her twin sister. The two had never been parted like they were now.

Her brothers had settled in Oakland, which had a booming shipping industry in which all the men worked. Laura and her young daughter found themselves on a Greyhound bus headed out from Eugene, Oregon, to Oakland, California. Laura was prepared to sit in the rear of the bus as that was customary in Texas. Much to her surprise, no such rule existed here. She was shy and albeit uncomfortable when she was offered a seat in the middle of the coach. Her heart raced traveling without her husband. She had diapers and food and she had herself for this was all the baby needed. Laura, nineteen, wasn't by nature a shy person. In fact, she was quite the opposite. She had a way of putting people at ease. Her smile, like her laughter, was contagious. At home, she was the daughter who brought life to the household.

Settling into her seat, with you—baby Anna Mary—on her lap, Laura watched the countryside pass by. Everything was so very green. The west was very different from Texas. Clint had told her to keep to herself on the bus. He had warned her that people might want to talk to her. Laura laughed to herself. If anyone gave her the time of day she would talk with them. She loved her little daughter, but she couldn't talk to her. Laura feared she would be bored to death by the time the bus made it to Oakland. She thought back to her husband working, building the railroad in Oregon.

While she was happy to see her family, Laura was more than a bit worried. Clint was young, strong, and good looking. She hoped he would finish their home sooner than later. She did not want any women taking too kindly to him. It would be four years before Laura and her daughter would rejoin her husband.

My own beginnings differed from yours. I was created out of a violent act of rape, of incest. I was a constant reminder of the shame you and the family endured. It was widely known your father touched you, even though no one intervened. You were left unprotected, an unwilling participant of his violence.

Once over the shock of my skin color, translucent milky white with soft pink cheeks, you loved me. You protected and cherished me, dressing me in frilly clothing, sheltering me from the light of the sun. Week after week you took me to Children's Hospital where doctors, who thought me to be the perfect research material, poked and prodded me, never offering you any knowledge you could place hope in. You told me once that a doctor said I would either be a genius or an imbecile. I choose to see myself as a genius. Together we would learn how best to take care of me. You quickly discovered that like your first child I was curious about the world around me. I walked early according to all accounts, toddling after Greg, three years my senior. By the time I was four, I could read, learning an entire new world existed—one that I could become a part of.

I always felt a little separate from Greg and Felecia. I remember once when we lived on Wells Street that Grandfather came over to visit. He came to visit a lot. He would gather me onto his lap. I had to be under five. He would stroke my back, telling me I was Granddaddy's special girl. I loved being his special girl then. These little moments of sitting on his lap were the precursor to him raping me as a teenager.

Even with all I knew, I could not protect myself against him. I was terrified of him, of his violence. I too became pregnant, yet unlike you I had an abortion, stopping the cycle of women in our family bearing his children. You know, I never talked to you about how I felt having the abortion. It was the day after Thanksgiving, and you took me to the hospital. My stomach was empty, which was good because I could not have kept food down anyhow. I was scared and humiliated. You never believed me when I told you your father had made me pregnant. You said I was a liar. I hated you for your blindness. I had had no reason to lie to you. Boys didn't even know I existed. I was too different.

The abortion hurt me deeply. Everyone in the family knew I had one. This knowledge embarrassed me, made me feel like a failure. More than thirty years later I still recall the statement you made that sealed my hatred of you. "If you were so damn smart, why didn't you keep from getting pregnant?" It was more a statement than a question. What bothered me more than anything was that I knew you had been touched by him, and I knew how much you detested that time in your life, and yet, and yet you did nothing to protect me. You did nothing but cast me out to the biggest, baddest wolf I have ever known. Why did you allow him to take my innocence away? Why could you not stand up to him and tell him to back off, to leave your children alone? Why?

I believe you were still afraid of your father. I believe he held some sort of power over you even in your adulthood that prevented you from taking charge of the situation. I believe you were a coward. I believe you were too chicken shit to protect your own. In this, I am not like you in the least. I would rather die than allow anyone to harm my daughter. She is more precious to me than life itself. Even now in her adolescence when she is often short with me, not talking to me more than is absolutely necessary because she prefers Lynn over me, I would kill, I would do time to protect her. Would I be terrified? Yes, of course I would be, yet I take a stand for those I love. I go to battle for what is mine. You didn't even try.

After the abortion, when you beat me with an extension cord, I feared and resented you. You took your anger out on me when you should have been comforting me. Instead you beat me as punishment for making your life difficult. Well, fuck that. Again, it was me who dealt with the shame of the beating. I was the one who tried to hide the welts and bruises.

I was called into the nurse's office and questioned as to why I was walking oddly. I was the one who shook with terror when Child Protective Services were called in. I was the one who watched you meet with the social worker in our living room. I watched you talk your way out of being penalized for harming me. When I heard the social worker say I was staying with you, I knew I would not love you again. I would not trust you again. I would not believe in you again. It was then I made up my mind to do whatever I needed to do to go to college, to leave your home so I never had to have your life.

I thought the abortion would be the end of the incest. Grandfather just became more careful. The incest stopped when I left for college. It stopped because when I was home on break I had the courage to say no. Shaking with rage, I told him he would never touch me again. It stopped because I was courageous. I had the power to threaten him. I would speak out. I would tell the police. I was slapped for that one, but it was worth it. He never touched me again. For a time, I stopped coming home. It was easier. It was safer.

I was ill equipped for the world, in part due to having been molested. I was ill equipped because I was timid. I'd been terrified most of my life, and I knew nothing about what healthy relationships could be like. I'd observed that women were independent, they worked, they raised children, maintained a home, and put up with men who were less than honorable. No, thank you.

When I began to want my own children, I could not bear them. My body in self-preservation caused my uterus to look like a giant crater with adhesions protruding into and embedded in the uterine wall. There was no place safe for a fetus to grow inside me. I believe the body is smarter than the brain. My body knew I needed to be protected. My body knew I would stop the cycle of incest babies. Once again, my body betrayed me.

For as long as I can remember, I have always wanted to have a child who looked like me. I wanted to have a baby with albinism. With my albino genes to contribute to the mix, I was guaranteed at least a chance. When I discovered I could not bear children, I cried. I cried because I knew the abortion had something to do with it. It wasn't logical, but in my heart I knew it. To this day I don't have any confirmation of whether or not the abortion I had at fifteen affected my ability to have babies. All I know is what my intuition tells me. It's funny, because I still managed to become a mommy. I just had to work around the problem.

Working around problems . . . seeking solutions . . . I learned from you. You taught me that I could have whatever I wanted if I put my mind to it and was willing to do the work to get there. So I did what any determined woman would do. I started researching adoption. I know that God and the ancestors were looking out for me because we, Lynn and I, had the smoothest nine-week adoption process ever. Our friends would leave baby things on our doorstep, clothing, toys, a crib, all discovered after a day working with other people's children. Everything happened quickly, easily, and thankfully without hitch.

The first time you saw Jewel you beamed with joy. You had to see for yourself that she had ten fingers and ten toes. You knew about babies. I was the amateur. I hovered over you as you removed her dress and onesie, then replaced the dress as it was 25 degrees warmer than at our home by the ocean. You held your newest granddaughter with pride. You were finally complete with knowing that I had become a mother. Your smile could be seen from across the room as you held our week-old Jewel. Word of our arrival traveled quickly through the house, which had been transformed into a cool, quiet, indoor haven for the grandmothers and a lovely garden celebration for everyone else.

We emerged from the bedroom, you carrying the baby and I close at your side. Unable to stand my hovering any further, you handed the contented child over to me. We were enveloped with love and greetings from everyone. We were overwhelmed at how many people had come to welcome Jewel into our family. When Jewel did finally sleep, she would do so in a new bassinet surrounded by all the grandmothers—you, who would be called Grandma Ann. Carol, my second mother, who would become Nonna for Jewel. Ginger, now called Ama, named by Jewel. Liz, though not a mom but a fantastic aunt. Grammy, Andrea's mom who was as giddy as you were. And of course Lynn and I periodically checking in just in case she woke. That day you and Jewel were the stars. You were the congratulated grandmother and she the much-awaited, longed-for child of your child. We were three generations then, four counting your mother still alive then. Like you, like me, Jewel has been loved and cherished.

Our lives are parallel, yours and mine. Becoming a mother helped me to understand some of what you experienced being my mother. I would be on my way somewhere, waiting for a bus and I would find myself questioned by strangers as to whether or not I was her mother. Jewel in the carrier or on my hip, hand possessively on my neck, my face, was clearly mine. Yet people just saw the difference in our skin tones and made an assumption. Frequently I was assumed White or I had been with a Black man. The first few times I paid these interactions no mind. Then I became irritated at peoples' ignorance. I wondered during these interactions what your life must have been like with me. You were younger than I was as a mother. You had other children who needed you just as much, and yet you had me, a child who needed so much more attention, so much more care. I learned compassion those first years. I learned how to see a snapshot of life through your eyes. Other times I would return home incensed. "How dare they question me and my baby," I would tell Lynn, Jewel's other Mama. Lynn always knew what to say to calm me.

At night, after getting Jewel to bed, I would sit thinking about how hard life must have been for you. I recall asking you how you dealt with all the doctors' visits, all the covering me up, watching me bump into walls, fall on my face because I didn't see a step, and so on. Comparatively speaking, my life was a cakewalk. I knew how to deal with people because I had grown up watching you do so. I knew when to educate and when to tell folks to back off. I knew how to stake claim to what was mine.

Now I am in uncharted territory. I parent a teenager. Unlike me, my daughter is popular and social. She is confident and knows how to work a room. She is safe and secure, loved and cherished. She is valued for who she is as an individual. She is free of the wolf. Like you, I find myself wanting to escape this stage of Jewel's development, and at the same time I miss the closeness we had just a year or so ago. Lynn has become the preferred parent because she speaks "teenager." I don't. I speak zero through age 12 it seems. I find myself checking out with music or the computer. You also used music to escape. When music no longer worked, drugs became your escape. I think the difference is that when Jewel wants to talk or just be in the same room with me, I stop what I'm doing and make myself available. The world is different now for kids. There is more pressure, both internal and external. There are more expectations. So I find my way with her. I take shortcuts into her language. I find ways to have quality time with her. I find time to not lose my mind. Like you, I leave home when I need to. I go see Carol to get my mom time. When you gave me over to Carol as a young woman, you were selfless. You knew what you could and could not give me. You knew I needed more. Giving Carol to me and me to her has been a priceless gift to us both. It is due to you both I am the woman I am today. I have been imprinted upon by each of you. I love that. I love that you were generous with someone who took such great interest, care, and love for me. Thank you.

I've been examining our family history. I look at old photographs of you, of the Lester women, of myself with Greg and Felecia. Somehow I don't have any family pictures of all of us with Clinton. Interesting. I have reached the point where I can tell the truth about my parentage. I am no longer ashamed to have been the product of rape and incest. When I share this with people, I find they are unprepared. They are not sure of what response to have. Neither am I. I have had to do a great deal of personal work to get to this point. I have made peace with my demons. I wish you had been courageous enough to confront yours. I wish you could have been stronger. I wish you were still alive. And yet, you are not living. I must find my way without you. And I do, find my way that is. I now know where I belong. This family I grew up in is simply one branch of my tree. We are all different and yet the same.

Recently I've been examining our family trees along with photographs. I am fortunate to have information from both the Eastmans and the Lesters. When the envelope came in the mail, I left it on a small table in my living room. I walked by the manila envelope more times than I can count. Ultimately, I surrendered. Bringing the envelope into the bedroom, I opened it, taking my magnifying glass out so I could see the information clearly. I think more than anything I was struck by the word unknown written in for my father on the family line. He is not unknown. Maybe, they, family, are just waiting for me to name the truth. Hmm.

I find myself sitting uncomfortably, rubbing my hands together at the thought of naming the truth. While I am not ashamed to state the truth, I still have a knot of tension in my belly. I still want to run from the room and distract myself from my feelings. And yet here I sit. Wanting to act out, my thoughts range from why do they need to know and it's none of their business anyhow, to, well, here we go again, opening my own special can of worms. Now at 47, I choose to revisit that can, emptying out the contents for all to see.

I also reflect on what my life might have been like if I, like you, had birthed a child at fifteen. Would I have loved my son or daughter? Would my spirit have gone into hiding as tongues wagged in judgment? If by some twist of fate the child had been born with albinism, how would I have felt? Would I have been able to make a life for us? Would I have managed to leave home? Would I develop exasperation and ambivalence toward my child because she was just one more generation adding to the countless notches on Grandfather's belt of bastard offspring?

These are questions I ask myself. When I am honest, able to stand in my truth, I know I would have had a far more challenging life. More to the point, in these moments I have compassion for you. I am more forgiving of you as I understand that while we experienced similar brutality, I escaped and broke the cycle of abuse. That while my spirit was for a time in hiding, it has emerged and I am now whole. I have the life I do, in part because of you. Unable to defend yourself or your children, you pushed me out into the world, demanding that I succeed.

LOSING MOTHER

We had returned from a rare evening out, paid the babysitter, and chatted with her until her mother arrived. Only then did I check the messages on the phone. At the sound of my nephew's voice, my heart nearly stopped. I knew the message was about Mother. She was always in need of something. She's not old, but the last sixteen months had been brutal. Her parents died three months apart. Grief, overpowering grief, numbed her. Daily crack cocaine had debilitated her. Mother was a walking shell. Instead of listening to a recording, I dialed the house. As I waited for my eldest nephew to answer, my movement limited by the length of the phone cord, still I paced. I told myself I'd be better off standing tapping my foot. My mind raced, imagining what mess I might need to clean up.

"Grandma Ann is in the hospital. She fell and is in a coma." Tears stung my eyes as my throat tightened, wanting to let loose a scream. Numbly I managed that I'd be there as soon as I could. I'm not sure how long I sat at the kitchen table. I know

I called my mother's sister, my favorite aunt, who was due to arrive the next day. She would be attending Grandparents' and Special Friends Day at my daughter's school. I walked down the long hallway to our bedroom. Tears streaming down my face, I told my partner of twelve years what was going on. Leaving our sleeping daughter with her Ama, the grandmother she saw daily, we drove to Oakland.

Highland Hospital scares me. It is the county hospital where all traumas are brought to. You have to go through security just to gain admittance to the elevators. What frightens me most is the ever present threat of violence. Victims of senseless shootings brought in and the possibility of retaliation drive-bys on site. The desperation of people who cannot afford insurance and who must wait sometimes for hours just to be seen for something that could be remedied if they had a physician. I think also there's just an energy there that makes me really, really uncomfortable. Once we are cleared, we head to ICU where Mother is.

The first face I see as I stand in the entry to Mama's room is my grandmother's twin sister, which just pisses me off. What I love most about my beloved is her calm in the middle of chaos. She is formidable at just over five feet. Built like a wrestler, my family tends to give her a wide berth. Tonight I am grateful for her quiet power. Sighing deeply, I do what I can to put a clamp on my attitude. My great aunt is a bully. There's no sugar coating it. When Grandmother died, my aunt bulldozed her way into her sister's house with her son, badgered my mother into giving her many of grandmother's prized possessions, including the stunning hat collection. I had taken the mink months before along with other treasures Grandmother decided I should have and those I was to keep in trust for her great granddaughters.

My first instinct was to demand to know from my great aunt why she was there. Perhaps my aunt was present out of guilt or obligation. Maybe it was all she felt she could do for her late sister. Either way, I wasn't thrilled to see her. I waged the first of several subsequent inner battles, concluding this one wasn't worth the energy. I greeted her with the perfunctory kiss upon her cheek. She rose, saying she'd be back the next day. Only after she'd left did I allow myself to take a closer look at Mama.

The first thing I observed as I stood at the head of the bed, leaning over her, were the burns on her face. "What the hell?" I whispered. I held her hand, the skin cracked and brittle. Hers was the hand of an old woman, but Mama wasn't old. Tears flooded my eyes, blurring my vision. What the hell happened to my mother? Even as I asked myself the question I already knew the answer.

Lifting the bedcovers I inspected Mama's legs and feet. They were dry and ashy. The sound of chattering machines filled the room. My beloved sat in a chair watching me, book on her lap. She had both of her parents. This was new territory for her. She knew I needed answers and squeezed my hand as I exited the room.

My stomach is in knots as I sit in a staff room off the nurses' station. They're being evasive about Mama's condition, and I don't understand. I told them I was her eldest daughter. On some level, I understood it wasn't their fault about what could and could not be disclosed to me. My mind was racing. What did I know about Mother's health history? As I looked from one person to the other, I knew I had to make a hunch.

"I know about the HIV." I forced myself to breathe. Even as I'd said the words I knew they were true. There was a collective sigh. "Oh, shit," was all that kept going through my head. "You see," the male nurse began, "we just can't tell family members that information unless they already know." Inside, my brain and my body were reeling. I had garnered information out of them on a fucking hunch. Part of me wanted to pat myself on the shoulder for being so damned clever. The other part of me was mortified.

My mother was no saint. In fact, her life had been extremely challenging. Her parents had never let her go physically or emotionally. Even after their deaths, they held her spirit captive. Mama had become a shadow of herself. Drugs had done that to her. Before the drugs, my mother had given her body away to others, never clear on the difference between sex and love. This was how she'd contracted HIV. I ceased listening. I returned to my mother.

I climbed onto the bed with her, curling myself around her and cried. I cried for all the regret I felt behind not seeing her more.

I cried for what would be a life cut too short. I cried because I was losing my mother and I still so very much needed her.

The aroma of fresh coffee roused me hours later. I hadn't remembered falling asleep. Carefully I disentangled myself from my mother's comatose body. Sitting on the edge of the bed, coffee in hand, I started making a mental list of what I needed to do and who I needed to call. It was still dark, so I figured it was around 5 a.m. Lynn had been busy as I'd slept. There was an overnight bag sitting on the floor next to her.

"I figured you'd be out for a while, and I was right. So, I went home to get you some things."

"I am so lucky and so loved," I told her. After placing food in my hand and letting me know my cell phone was fully charged and that there was a roll of quarters in one of the pockets of my coat, she left to get our daughter off to school.

Alone, save for the company of my unconscious mother and the whir of machines keeping her alive, I thought what a mess this would be. I knew my family would act out. There was no way around it. There had been so much loss in such a short time. First the grandparents, gone within three months of one another, and now Mother a year later. I had to see my sister. Mother's wishes were clear. She had told us over and over again from the time we were teenagers that if she had no quality of life we needed to let her go. I began to shake, tears staining my cheeks again. I hugged myself, rocking back and forth. I hated being the responsible one. Yet I was cognizant that hatred was futile because I had been responsible for so very long. Why should this time be any different?

Finally, a doctor showed up. After examining the monitors and the chart, he asked me to join him outside the room. I was told Mama would not emerge from the coma. That at this point there was no brain activity. No brain activity? No, no, no, I said over and over in my head. We would have to make a decision. I told him I needed to speak with my sister and could we meet with the team later that day? Mama's sister would be arriving later that day from the Pacific Northwest.

And thus, the day progressed. Clients had been called, informed of my family situation. Reassurances to not worry about work. Women from the organization I volunteered for were contacted to fill in for me on calls and in some cases to take over for me while I focused on my family. These things were handled by rote, as a few years previous I'd had to do the same thing though the circumstances had been different. With my affairs handled, once again I sat on a chair, my head resting on the bed. I slept.

It was a month before. January 2003. I'd gone to Oakland to see Mama. She was high as usual. Talking fast and quickly ushering me upstairs so I wouldn't see what she was doing. I was no longer naive as I had once been. She was happy to see me. Looking around the house, I noticed some of Grandmother's possessions were absent. The silver tea set, her prized crystal vase gone. My heart sank. Sold or traded for drugs. Mama had moved into Grandmother's bedroom. Two years earlier, she had a stroke and used a walking cane. Living upstairs was a good thing. It meant the kids could watch over her.

I found it difficult spending time in the house. It held far too many traumatic memories for me to ever be at ease.

Mama and I sat on the big bed that took up most of the bedroom. She told me she was doing well. I knew she wasn't. I hadn't slept well for much of the year. Because of our intuitive bond, I knew she wasn't sleeping either. The deep circles beneath her eyes showed me this. She was thin, and her legs and feet were ashy.

Lost in my own thoughts, I hadn't heard Mama say she would be right back until she repeated it a second time. Sure, sure, I nodded. While she was gone, I called my eldest nephew into the room for a real update. As suspected, Mama wasn't sleeping or eating. She smoked crack, and she cried. She wasn't taking her medication.

"Go get your Mama," I angrily decreed. He fled the room. As much as I hated to see Mama in pain, I hated to see my entitled sister show up ready for a fight even more. Felecia felt she was always in my shadow. We had been compared to each other all our lives, and I too bore resentment from the exercise.

It was Felecia's job to make sure Mama took her meds. It was her job to make sure Mama ate. This had been the agreement. This is why she lived rent free in the house with her children. And she wasn't doing her fucking job.

"Hey, sis," came the falsely sweet voice of my sister.

"Hey, yourself," I called back, doing my best to keep myself in check. "So, I hear Mama isn't doing what she's supposed to. I thought we agreed you would make sure she did." I watched her demeanor change from false joy to the crossing of her arms to the shift in her voice to a harder tone. Here we go, I thought.

"You think it's easy to make her do anything she doesn't want to do? She gone do what she will."

"I see you have no trouble helping her get high." I thought Felecia just might hit me. She whirled around so quickly. I shifted in my stance just in case.

"That's right, baby. I sure can. I make sure I get mine first. Just so you know Mama is sick."

Was this meant to derail me? "Sick with what?"

Felecia shrugged her shoulders. "You need to ask her that," she said, walking away. "She won't tell you. She had a stroke."

I didn't wait to find out more. "I hate this place," I muttered to myself. "It's not the same without Grandmother." Opening the bedroom closet, more things were missing. It doesn't matter, I told myself. It's just stuff. I sent word downstairs that I was leaving. And like always Mama emerged, her face worried. I hugged her, letting her know I had to go. I had to get back to the city before it grew too late. I didn't like being on public transit in the later evening. I tried to keep my voice light, but I could feel the tears threatening. She hugged me fiercely, just a little too hard, and I let her.

With hugs from my sister's boys and my usual gift of a few dollars to each, I was at the door ready to flee the battle zone. At the door, Mama pushed photo albums into my hands, insisting I take them for safe keeping. I knew not to argue. For the last two years, each time I came over I left with more than I brought. Last month, right before Christmas, I came home with the good silver. Was this how things were to be? Heirlooms parceled out to me whether or not I wanted or needed them? "Okay, Mama, I will take them home." Down the rickety grey steps I went, eyes alert to the goings-on of the block. I stood for a moment just looking at the house. I'm not sure why. Maybe I thought I wouldn't get the chance to do so again. Turning away, I made my way toward home.

This time I awoke to voices talking. I sat up, tension and soreness in my back and shoulders from the uncomfortable hospital chair. Felecia had arrived. As I stood, I saw the sadness all over her face. We held each other, past angers forgotten, for a long time. I am taller than she is, and when I opened my eyes still holding onto Felecia, the hall was filled with family. I could also see nurses hovering around the edge of the assembled crowd. There were far too many people here for the ICU floor, and I knew it.

"Hey," I whispered, "let's get most of these people out of here. The nurses are getting nervous. Plus, we have a meeting to go to." With the help of the eldest grandchildren, our family left the ICU, gathering instead outside in the parking lot.

We held hands, walking into the windowless conference room. There were a lot of people there. I hadn't realized Mama had these many doctors. Her condition was explained to us again. We learned she had a fever of 106 degrees and it was getting higher. I had never heard of a person's body temperature being so high. Her brain was being cooked. There was no way she could recover from that kind of injury. Mama was already gone. My sister began to cry. "We have to honor what she would want," I told her gently but firmly. "We have to let her go, right?"

We were both in tears. The doctors waited.

Once the paperwork was done, we returned to the ICU. We were met immediately by the same two nurses I had seen the night before. Mama had been moved to a corner room away from the business of the floor to accommodate the family being able to say goodbye. I thanked them as we were directed to the room. They needn't have bothered because as we approached the room we couldn't even get inside for the number of people there before us.

I got mad. Our eldest niece was having a meltdown. Why were some of these folks even here? Most of them hadn't bothered to see Mama since she'd lost her own mama, so why now? Damn looky-loos.

"Look, Earl, get T out of here. At least get her calmed down a bit." Felecia was bossy, and I knew the kids would listen to her.

As for everyone else . . . I get to be the bitch, I thought. Okay, fine. I looked at them all, saying nothing. Taking a deep breath, I gathered myself. "We need some privacy to be with our mother. I know you all love her, but we need to be with her now." I didn't care how my words sounded. They all needed to leave.

I sat, my back to the sun-filled window, watching the nurses detach all the equipment from Mama. My sister was gone. She said she just couldn't be there to watch Mama die. My job. An hour later, Lynn showed up with Aunt Rosie. She had changed her flight. Thank God for small miracles. Once more, there was a group of relatives in the room as well as the hospital chaplain. I was called out to meet with him. I resented his intrusion. I told him we had several ministers within the family at our disposal, intentionally dropping names. He left.

With the setting of the sun, my aunt and I found ourselves alone with Mama. Like me, she had unfinished business with her sister. I listened while Auntie talked about when they were girls. I listened while she prayed and quietly cried. We talked to each other, took turns applying lotion to her battered skin. I had no explanation for the burns. I later learned Mama had fallen into the fireplace one day after building a fire. Why in the world had she been making a fire? I wondered. I'll deal with that later, I told myself. Around eleven thirty we decided to head back to my place for some sleep as it seemed Mama was hanging in there strong. She had been off life support for eight hours. Her heart was strong, though her body temperature continued to climb. No sooner had we settled in than the telephone ring. The hospital. We drove back, making the trip in less than a half hour.

The lights were low in the room. I could hear Mama breathing shallowly, her body occasionally twitching. I wondered if she was rallying and knew she wasn't. Once again, I curled up beside her, placing my head on her chest so I could hear her heart beat. I knew this would be the last time I would have her this close to me. Auntie wrapped herself in a blanket. We waited.

I used to have this fear about being alone, dying alone. I was terrified. I would tell myself, I will be married. I will be with someone and when the time comes for me to die I will not be alone. I was so naive. While I sat watch, waiting for my mother to release her last breath, I came to understand that we begin life alone and we end life alone. No one can make that journey with or for us.

At 4 a.m. Friday, February 14th, 2003, Mama let go. I felt her final breath set itself free, and she was gone.

We watched as the nurses did their final examination. By then I was exhausted and numb. We left the hospital in the predawn. During the drive home, we would occasionally talk, but mostly we kept to our own thoughts. I had called Felecia. That was all I could do.

The interesting thing about losing someone is that your own life continues. There is still work, there are still your children. There is still life. Somehow Auntie pulled off going to Grandparents and Special Friends day at school. We opted not to tell Jewel as we didn't want to upset her. She was so thrilled in having her great aunt in attendance for the special day at school.

The telephone rang nonstop. There were a multitude of details to be handled. From meeting with the funeral home to meeting with my great uncle who would officiate the funeral. The one thing I could not do was return to the house on Holly Street. I feared what the house had become. And I didn't want to see the place if it had been stripped of the things that made the place a home. Plus, it held too many memories.

The backyard was where I first learned how to grow green beans, tomatoes, and collard greens. How to tend to them, talk to them, nurture them, and ultimately reap their harvest. In that house was where I'd been cared for at seven when I was affected by chicken pox, mumps, and German measles back to back. The kitchen was where I patiently sat on a stool and watched Grandmother cook and listened to her sing. This was where we had lived once the grandparents moved to the house on the hill. This was where I had my first kiss, where I confessed I was pregnant, where I was raped and molested. I had no love for this house. This was the place of many holiday dinners, even more Sunday dinners filled with laughter. This was where I sat as a teenager listening to my mother, exhausted, telling the police to just keep my big brother. That she wasn't coming for him this time. This was the house I had fled as soon as I could. I had no love for this house.

After Mama died, I became angry. One day I left the house, telling no one, to take a walk. I needed to get out. We were living with my mother-in-law, and there was no privacy. I was more than angry. I was incensed. I had so much rage toward my sister, it was leaking all over my life. I was short with my seven-year-old and with my beloved. I was miserable. I called a friend. I needed to talk to someone who I didn't need to explain the family history or dynamics to. She let me vent and cry and rage. By the time I was done, I had walked to Ocean Beach, which was two miles from home.

I am sure people who passed me saw me crying. In fact, I know they did. No one intervened. I recall my friend telling me that crack eats your soul. I believe her. I watched my mom transform from a functional person to a shell. I witnessed her lose herself because her personal demons were too overwhelming to face head on. If I was honest, I could and did see the progression of her demise. From the loss of her innocence by her father's hand to her parents never really letting her go to have her own life, to the loss of her youngest child to the discovery of cocaine then crack because through the haze she could breathe. But I kept coming back to the thought that my sister was supposed to take care of her and she hadn't. "Could Felecia not do anything!" I heard myself scream into the receiver. "She had one goddamned job, and she couldn't even do that successfully." I was hurting so deeply. I had lost my mama. I was lost. Who was going to help me with Jewel? Who would guide me when I hit those parenting rough spots?

As I ambled home from the beach, I was hit with another boulder. I was alone. I had no parents. I was an orphan. I cried more. Could this day get any worse? Please. The house was in an uproar when I walked in.

"Mommy! Mommy, where were you?" came my daughter, breathless. No sooner had she asked the question, she was skipping down the long hall to the sunroom. "Mama, I found Mommy." Instead of following Jewel to join the rest of our small family, I walked through the dining room into the kitchen, turning on the kettle for tea. Lynn quietly entered the sunny room. I squared my shoulders, preparing for the worst.

All she said was, "I was worried. I didn't know where you had gone. Don't do that again."

For a moment I stared, facing her, just taking her words in. Lynn had been very understanding, very supportive. She was right. I had been irresponsible. I turned to apologize, my words uttered to empty space. Lynn had left the room. I sat at the old melamine table for hours. Later, curled up in bed, I apologized. I told Lynn about my rant-filled conversation. I had walked four miles, a portion of my grief. That night I slept a dreamless sleep.

MOTHERING

I have two mothers. I was birthed and raised by one, and sent off to the finishing school by the other. I now refer to Carol as mom. She has and continues to love me, push me, encourage me, as well as tell me hard truths when I need them. Mom is the woman I go to when I am troubled or when I need to bounce ideas off of someone.

When I met my partner in the fall of 1990, before I decided to date her we went to dinner at my folks' home so Mom could assess Lynn's character. Thankfully, she passed the test. Five years later when faced with being unable to conceive, Lynn and I turned to adoption as we really wanted to be parents. Again, Mother and Mom were there. I had learned of an unborn child that needed a home. A different family had backed out of the adoption. Excited and terrified, I made a phone call that altered our lives forever. Yet again, Mom was there offering encouragement and support.

"If this is what you want, then let's make this happen." That is how Mom is. She assesses, analyzes, and takes action. During one of many conversations we had while Lynn and I were navigating the adoption process, Mom told me, "I won't have you give up on your dream of being a mom. I had given up on my dream until you came into my life."

I held the telephone in speechless amazement. Tears streamed down my face. "Wow, Mom," I managed. "I had no idea."

"How could you? I never admitted this out loud to anyone."

This is the nature of our relationship. Mom and I share things with each other. Deep things. I have been profoundly affected having her as my mom. My albinism has never been an issue for her. Mom has always seen well beyond my physical attributes. I have learned immeasurable skills from her, for which I am eternally grateful. Coupled with the childhood lessons I learned from Mother, I am an unstoppable force.

I chose to become a parent consciously. Given the configuration of my relationship, I knew becoming pregnant would be a challenge. I would learn that the actual challenge for me would be accepting I was unable to conceive. Faced with significant reproductive issues, I had a heart-to-heart with myself and subsequently with my partner. I concluded that my body had chosen to protect itself as a result of having been molested. I asked myself what was more important—being a mom or carrying a baby? Being a mom won out. I knew through experience that babyhood goes by quickly.

The path to adoption was far from easy. I had to grieve the loss of bearing a child. I knew there would be no one who would resemble me.

I wanted an African American child. I knew we would be good parents. Ten short weeks after making the initial telephone call to our adoption agency, Lynn and I packed our bags, took off our commitment rings, and headed off to bring home our baby girl.

I loved being a mom. I adored my daughter. I cherished each stage and milestone achieved. What I did not love was how other people I encountered regarded and made assumptions about me. I interpreted their expressions as, "She can't possibly be yours." I began to understand how my own mother must have felt when she was young and with me. The irony is that the majority of rude comments and incredulous looks came from other Black people. It was as though they could not see beyond skin color. Could they not see my features? These encounters angered me, made me want to swear at people, and made me fiercely protective of my daughter. These same emotions were what I knew Mother had endured. And very much like my mother, I dared anyone to doubt the validity of who I was.

Parenting on a good day can be a challenge. Parenting as a visually impaired individual is an ongoing adventure. I constantly had to remind myself that my daughter was body smart. She was in fact more agile than I could imagine. One month before her fifth birthday, my daughter, along with another child, was hit by a driver who ran a red light. Our family was devastated.

We rallied together, surrounding Jewel with love and nurturing. That summer there was a meet and greet at a local park for parents and new students for her elementary school. Jewel still had the hardware attached to her leg. We lovingly called her the Borg Princess. Having a broken leg did not stop my girl. I marveled as she climbed and subsequently slid down a high slide. Even with her leg healing, my girl held body confidence. When asked why we allowed her to climb or even play at all with an injured leg, my partner and I responded, "As if we could stop her." While I too was terrified my five-year-old might potentially fall and reinjure her leg, I could not allow that fear to stop her. What I could not see, I knew my partner Lynn could. This is how we chose to parent.

I learned to trust and use my senses when it came to being a mom. I still do. When children are small, we are up close and personal with them. We notice everything, and I mean everything. From the newest bruise to the latest milestone. It is only as they grow and become mobile we must pay attention differently. This has been my experience. I could tell if my daughter was content or unhappy by watching her body language. If she was within sight, by listening to how she walked and the sound of her voice. I could sense frustration, sadness, or joy. I called it mom sense. She called it annoying.

Once our children become adults, parenting takes on a new course. I believe I am part mom and part life coach. I listen, I guide, I love her unconditionally. We have a relationship where she can divulge anything to me. Jewel trusts that I will handle my own emotions separate from her.

This was certainly the case when after 24 years I left my relationship with her other mom. I recognized the importance of keeping my side of the street clean. My daughter wasn't breaking up with us, we were doing that with one another. This clarity on my part enabled Jewel to have her own process, to develop individual relationships with each of her parents.

After Mother died, it was Mom who reassured me she wasn't going anywhere. That in fact, I possessed one remaining parent. Mom is fond of saying that I am an apple born of two trees. This is accurate. I possess mannerisms and characteristics from them both. I have Mother's love of literature and writing. I have Mom's adventurous spirit. I have been gifted with pragmatism, independence, an appreciation for good food, and a love of life.

Conversely, I recognize that they are my mirrors. And that, similar to them, I tackle bouts of insecurity, self-doubt, fear of success, and issues of trust. I am not unique. Many people battle these issues daily. The difference is that unlike my mother, I've examined mine with a magnifying glass, ensuring I assess the fine details and nuances so that I can continue to thrive.

NOAH CONFERENCE 2014

This past winter I made the decision to attend the NOAH conference for the first time. I did so with intention, being fully committed no matter what. Once I make a decision, very little stops me. Lodgings booked, I then waited for registration to open. Of course, once I could I did in fact register. For years I had stalked the NOAH website and later the Facebook page. Even though I wasn't yet a member, I felt compelled to keep an eye on what NOAH was up to, organizationally speaking of course. I was accustomed to being the only me. I had a couple of friends with albinism I had cultivated in my adulthood so I did not feel alone.

Fast-forward to July. As the conference quickly approached, the more my excitement grew. "I'm really doing this!" I would tell myself. Butterflies danced in my stomach, each fluttering of the wings propelling me forward. The night before I departed I could barely sleep. My family cheered me on as they were equally excited. I boarded my short flight to San Diego, trying not to think too hard. Epic fail, of course. My mind was full of questions. Would there be anyone there who looked like me? Would I be welcomed? Would the panel I was co-moderating go well? What if I hated the conference? "Enough!" I told myself. I had to believe all would work out well.

Upon arriving at the host hotel, I saw small groups of people chatting, making plans for outings and just catching up with one another. There were albino people everywhere. Oh, my God! I'm really here. I observed more closely, seeing children with albinism. I was so distracted I had to be called by the concierge to check in. I was already overwhelmed emotionally. My eyes stung with happy tears, tension left my body, and I reminded myself to breathe. I had come home.

I believe the biggest thing I came to see initially was the individuality within the group whole. We all have albinism, and we all are uniquely ourselves. We look similar, and yet our features, our characteristics, are our own. When I was young, I used to think that if I were in a crowd of several hundred people who looked like me I could blend in. I could be invisible. By Thursday evening, I found myself in a ballroom with hundreds of people with albinism. Children, oh my, there were so many children. While I would always be me, I understood I would never be invisible again.

As I walked through the ballroom seeking a seat, I took in the various shades of albinism. There were those who like me had very fair skin and white hair. There were those who were sun kissed, meaning they had that golden skin tone. There were those who were more ruddy in complexion. And they were all me. I marveled at families who seemed so very comfortable already. I regarded children after the opening session who ran through the room playing tag. While I only knew one other person there with albinism, my best friend, I would soon make dozens more.

As the evening came to a close, I knew I was not yet ready to sleep. So like many others I joined the growing congregation of folks out near the pool. The night was still warm, and the darkness was a welcome to my overextended eyes. We PWA's can be a reticent crowd. We are always in observer mode initially, assessing new situations and environments, getting the lay of the land, so to speak. This is also the case for me. Approaching the pool crowd, we were immediately welcomed. "Come on over. Here, have a seat. And enjoy the beverages on the table." I breathed easier. Like all first-timers, I was being enfolded into the community.

Friday morning, the workshops and panels began. I soaked up everything. I learned more about albinism from the research viewpoint, and my head was full with all the knowledge. Between workshops I continued to meet people. I know it's a cliche, but I truly felt like a child in a candy shop. Do I go to a workshop, or do I enjoy the conversation I am having with this parent who has a child with albinism? For the remainder of the weekend, I would do both. If a session called to me, I went. If I found myself having a conversation with someone, I stayed where I was. While the sessions were interesting and valuable, it was the personal interactions that held most precious value for me. I met parents, teens, and other people with albinism like myself. Conversations with my peers, mostly the ones that took place during the evenings while socializing, were wonderful. The exchange of information around technology, scopes, and other visual equipment and skincare opened my eyes to what I had been missing.

I was awestruck. That is the only way I can explain how I felt. During an outing on Friday, I found myself pulled by someone as our large group was divided in half. "You're with us." A simple statement that meant I was embraced and accepted, nearly made me cry. We were mixed ethnically and age-wise. Yet we were predominantly African American. We were ourselves, and we were one another. Our shared commonality of albinism was just that. We laughed. We were unruly, and we had so much fun. We were professionals and students. We were oblivious to how others in restaurants or on the street perceived us. Honestly, we didn't care because we were comfortable in our own skin.

The things that worried me before the conference became a non-issue. The panel I co-moderated went quite well. I arrived alone and departed with new friends. I enjoyed myself immensely, and I knew I would return for the next conference.

After the NOAH conference, I returned to my daily life, but I was changed. I had experienced an amazing weekend, met tons of new people, created new friendships. For the first time, I felt as though I had a community. I had a pack. A family. One morning I sat at my favorite before-work cafe reflecting on the conference. My mind was still awash with so many emotions and thoughts that I found it difficult to write. Suddenly I was slammed to my core.

I have fought for inclusion all my life. I cajoled my mother as a young child to be allowed to play outdoors with my brother and sister. A battle was fought on my behalf for me to attend regular school. Once in school, teachers advocated for me to have all the materials I needed to fully participate in my classes. I battled to have similar freedoms as my siblings. Tenaciously I pushed my intellect, knowing it was my exit from my home circumstances to a different life. When I was a young woman I demanded inclusion into the women of color, the lesbian of color community. My presence made some uncomfortable because they could not, would not, look beyond color. When my body told me no, I declared I would still become a mother. And I did. I am a scrapper. I am willful. I know that when there is something I want, I manage to somehow make it happen. So I was completely unprepared when 20 minutes before I was due at work I had an emotional meltdown. All the spiritedness, negotiation skills, and bravery in the world could not buffer me from myself that morning. As I cried, huge sobs wracked my body. I realized I had been alone. So very alone. Furthermore, I had grown so accustomed to being the only me in my world that I hadn't even known I was alone until I wasn't. Here was yet another aspect of my identity now awakened, requiring its place amidst the other layers of myself.

Albinism for me is an extension of who I am. In the same fashion being African American/Black and being a lesbian are also vital parts of me. Just as being a mother of a now college student and being in a committed relationship also define me in my community. I live my life in an all-encompassed way. And yet albinism has once again risen to the forefront. Well, that's not exactly true. Albinism, and my albinism in particular, has been very present for me in the last year as I have been working on my memoir. Attending the NOAH conference brought me to attention.

MAKING THE
INVISIBLE VISIBLE

"The notion that any African would discriminate against someone because of the color of their skin after what Black people around the world have gone through is crazy. It is infuriating, and I have no patience for it."

—President Barack Obama on the harvesting of albino body parts for ritual use[1]

It has been a lifetime journey for me to be able to say I love, embrace, and am proud of being a Black woman with albinism. Growing up never meeting another person with albinism caused me to feel isolated and without any role models. Now I

---

1   http://www.mrctv.org/videos/obama-harvesing-body-parts-fool-ish-tradition-africa?utm_campaign=naytev&utm_content=55c280f7e4b-06877c908a50a

am committed to being that woman who is an ally and model to others.

While I watched the video clip of Obama speaking against atrocities committed toward people with albinism, I was reminded of the hope, joy, and amazement I felt when we elected our first Black President in 2008. Culturally we were all so excited for the possibilities. President Obama represented progress and change. And to witness today how he addressed a cause so important to me brought forth those same emotions I had eight years ago. I'm overcome with happy tears. My heart swells with pride. He was clearly frustrated, struggling to contain his anger. His outrage on behalf of people with albinism throughout Africa made me weep.

The continued state of racism and vicious attacks on Black people in this country is what I and many others believe is domestic terrorism. This is at the forefront of my mind. Discussions and advocacy are important and imperative in order for people to learn how to tolerate, accept, and embrace difference.

What hasn't been talked about is the racism and invisibility that I have experienced as a white-skinned Black woman. I am not always seen for who I am. As a fifty-something woman with white hair, which is often hidden beneath a wide-brimmed hat, mostly, if at all, I'm viewed as an old White woman. Neither of which is true. The emotional and psychological impact is huge. I am also the victim of ageism, which is just another -ism used to deny me of being seen for who I am.

I am going to go out on a limb here and say that frankly I care not what White people think of me. I am accustomed to being mistaken for one of them. Honestly, when it is helpful I allow them to indulge in their assumptions because I gain preferred treatment. I have no shame in this. However, what has hurt me is being shunned by Blacks.

When I was a child, people constantly asked my mother whose child I was because they could not comprehend or accept that I was in fact hers. I watched her contain the same outrage our President displayed when confronted with people's ignorance. I was born at a time when little was known about albinism. So, my mother did what she needed to in order to buffer me from ill treatment. yet she could not protect me once I began school where I was required to make my own way socially.

As a young adult, I felt I constantly needed to prove my belonging whenever I attended events or sought to participate in Black-only space. Because I am visually impaired, I often failed to see the glares directed at me. However, I felt hostility. It was the occasional outspoken person who would ask why I was present. Always, I would state that I was Black. Always, I was disbelieved. Always, I wanted to slip away because my feelings were hurt. Sometimes I did. I was intimidated. Yet I continued to show up at events. In time, I became more confident and secure in my right to belong.

When I think of my African brothers and sisters with albinism, I am envious. The prevalence of albinism is greater in Sub Saharan Africa, especially in Tanzania where the ratio is 1/1400 as opposed to 1/18,000 here in the United States. Children do not experience the isolation of oneness as I did. There is shared experience and community. What PWA do live with is the fear of being attacked or killed and having their body parts harvested for ritual purposes. This too is racism. It is in fact worse because their lives are at stake. There is significant stigma at having a child with albinism. This has led to the creation of residential schools for children as a means of protection.

And so it is that in just a year I have cultivated a community for myself filled with PWA. This community is growing as I expand and form new friendships. Friendships are important, and contributing to community education and awareness holds equal value. I am one amongst many, speaking, advocating, and educating people about what life is like as a PWA and particularly as an African American person with albinism.

As I prepare to travel to Tanzania to attend the Pan African Albinism Conference, I do so with excitement and humility. For the first time, I will join with others who like myself are committed to making a difference in their communities. The thing that carries more weight is that I will be amongst people who look like me. When I think of this, I am moved so very deeply. Already, I have a sense of coming home. There is the known experience of understanding what it feels like to navigate as White in a culture of Brown, when culturally we are all Brown.

LOSING A CHILD
IN TANZANIA

There has been significant media coverage about atrocities toward persons with albinism in Tanzania. The aftermath of how families are affected has not received as much attention. Imagine your child has been placed for his/her safety in a Government Center or was attacked and did not survive. How would you feel? Imagine the impact on the remaining members of your family. The story I am about to share affected me deeply, both as a mother and as a woman with albinism.

I visited Lake View School in Mwanza District on the 25th of November 2015. After touring the school and meeting many wonderfully engaged students we returned to the administrative building. I was met by Peter Ash the founder and CEO of Under The Same Sun, UTSS. A woman by the name of Esther, whose child had been abducted in February if that year had arrived to be interviewed by him along with Vicky Ntetema the

Executive Director of the Tanzania UTSS office. I was invited to sit in on the interview.

First of all it is of the utmost importance to document the attacks as thoroughly as possible so that there is adequate concrete documentation to prosecute the attackers in court. The interviews are always difficult, just as this one was. I sat at a conference table listening taking notes. Peter and Vicky sat on either side of Esther. Vicky served as translator. Slowly Esther, a petite quiet woman, began to recount her story.

On a Sunday in February in the Geita region of Northwestern Tanzania Esther's husband was outside near the fire, several men entered the house where she and the children were. She was holding her small son Yohana who was eighteen months old.. The attackers tried repeatedly to wrench the baby from her. "It was like a tug of war." Esther conveyed. Frustrated by her refusal to let go of the child the attackers slashed her face with a machete, causing the skin, the face, to fall. Still she held on to her child. Next the machete was used on her arm. Only after the second injury was she forced to let go of the child. "I was powerless to hold him" she shared. Throughout the ordeal the abductors were silent. For a time she was unconscious. Once she was awake the remaking two children, one of whom also has albinism, begged to leave for fear of further attack. Holding the skin of her face up with one hand and the hands of her children with the other, they fled to neighbors who aided Esther in getting medical help.

Sorrow filled the room. Each person managed their reaction, some more effectively than others. "What kind of boy was Yohana? Was he happy? Did your other children love him?" Peter gently inquired. "Yes they loved him. They continue to be sad."

Esther was hospitalized for two months. During this time she underwent reconstructive surgery to repair her face and arm. Upon returning home she learned from her mother that the baby died. Esther's mother explained that Yohana's body was discovered in a shallow grave. His arms and legs had been hacked off.

There are more than 75,000 registered witchdoctors in Tanzania. The majority of whom believe that potions made from the body parts and hair of persons with albinism {PWA} can bring good luck, wealth and success. Body parts sell for tens of thousands of dollars. PWA in Africa face social stigma, alienation, and fear of being attacked. Sadly, family members sometimes aid these witchdoctors who hire men to abduct persons with albinism.

Yohana's father was eventually arrested in connection of his son's attack and murder.

When asked if she knew why her son was taken, Esther replied that she didn't know. Peter Ash then began to explain about albinism. Also affected with albinism, Peter shared that he was like Yohana and that albinism occurs throughout the world. I pulled up a photo on my phone of me as a child with my family. As I walked around the oblong conference table I was acutely aware that everyone was watching me. Standing before Esther, I pointed out my mother. She and her mother, who had accompanied her for the interview, marveled in surprise. They couldn't believe that I held similar resemblance to her late son and remaining daughter.

While in Tanzania I have found that most people have no idea I have albinism. Nor do they see me as American Black. Initially I was surprised, then I was hurt. I felt invisible. These emotions are not new to me. Growing up I struggled with my identity. While my family spanned the color spectrum, no one looks quite like me. Now I understand it is because many people, those with albinism included, have no idea that albinism occurs within other cultures or in other parts of the world.

At the end of the interview Peter conveyed his sadness for her loss, emphasizing that Johann was a good boy, a loved boy and valued in his family. Lastly Peter offered a prayer for Esther and her remaining children, whom Esther has not seen since the night of the attack. Both children were removed by authorizes. The daughter has been placed at a sanctuary for protection located on an island far away from the family. Her son has been placed in a government school. Esther had not seen her children in 9 months. I cannot imagine not seeing my daughter for that length of time. In addition to the physical pain she still experiences from her injuries, consider the emotional pain she feels as a result of losing one child and being separated from the remaining two.

As Esther and I said our goodbyes, our eyes locked. Hers held fatigue and sorrow. I also recognized love and appreciation. Esther stroked my face. In that moment the love and compassion I held for her was profound. A moment later she whispered "Mama" as we embraced.

The return drive to our hotel was quiet.Our driver sensed the somber mood and unlike earlier in the day, refrained from engaging us in conversation. I recalled conversations with my mother about her experience of toting me to and from doctors' visits. Memories of her handling rude and insensitive questions from strangers about me swirled in my head as did the many times she wiped tears away from my cheeks because someone had hurt my feelings with their words. My mother had been protective of her children, especially me, much in the same fashion as Esther had been in safeguarding her children. This innate need to do whatever was needed to ensure the freedom and care of their offspring and in this case at the expense of her own safety, bore confirmation for me as the fierceness of a mother's love.

MZUNGU

I have been traveling for a month, and today I begin the journey home. I am getting my hair braided before leaving Nairobi. Grey skies cast the illusion of cold. As I am driven, I gaze out the window, taking in gift shops stuffed with merchandise overflowing onto the sidewalk. A friend appears as the car pulls to the curb. She wears a blue wool coat, smiling as we embrace. We enter an alcove, which opens onto a path containing individual enclosed stalls. We reach our chosen shop, and I am introduced to a Masai man, the braider, who is eager to begin.

I have a lifetime relationship with my hair. My newborn head covered with a mass of soft white down, the texture of newly picked and cleaned cotton. Hair that required a delicate hand when it came to the straightening comb for it singed easily. Much like the man releasing tangles from my newly freed tresses, my mother showed no mercy. She had four children and didn't believe in catering to the emotions of her offspring. So rather than submit to her heavy-handed brand of comb wielding, I quickly learned to take charge of my head. As I sit outside of the shop, I wince as my hair is wrestled into submission.

Adults and children appear from booths to see the foreigner. Me. There's something rather freeing when I know I am being stared at. I am assumed mzungu or White person. This has been the case throughout my time in Tanzania and Kenya. I'm easily seen as American, but not as Black. I have white skin, and I have nappy white hair. Yet still I am not seen for who I am. The song from Rent goes through my head, the one where the lesbians are clearly about to break up at their commitment ceremony. Take me or leave me. This is how I feel, and I relax.

I'm midway to Paris. I've had fifteen hours to either embrace or reject my hairstyle. Interestingly as the braider was near to completing his task, my inner selves from young me to adult me each had an opinion about these Afro kink extensions. Occasionally I would peek into the mirror and witness brown hair where white should be. My inner five-year-old's fingers itched to explore them, and yet ingrained memory reminded me that we never ever touch a creation in progress for fear that wandering fingers would be gifted with the smack of the comb.

Thirteen-year-old me was caught in a time warp of remembering the initial hair coloring experience that was filled with skepticism and dread as I watched the splatter of brown hair color decorate the bath towel draped across my shoulders. The twenty-something me was matter of fact. "If I hate it, I can just take the extensions out." The seasoned adult ultimately had the final word. No matter how I felt about the new do, I would thank and appreciate the man who spent nearly three hours on my hair and I would give him a tip. "Yes, ma'am," the various parts of me responded within my head. Besides, whatever I choose to do upon returning home was my business.

In an accessible washroom at Charles de Gaulle airport outside of Paris, I gaze at my reflection. I analyze the image before me. I am still the same me. The only difference is my hair. My face is tight. Fatigue, stress, and confusion the predominant features. I am thirteen all over again.

And so at the thirty-hour mark I decide that I hate this mass of fake brown Afro kink hair twisted into faux dreads. This is not me. In part, the color is to blame. I would have used something lighter, but this was all that was available in Nairobi. Equally at fault is the texture. When I run my hand across the twists, the coarseness is unbearable.

Tears sting my eyes. Revelation appears wielding a truth I tucked away. Inasmuch as I held excitement about being at a conference alongside people with albinism from African Nations, my greater hope was to be recognized as a person of color with albinism amongst my peers.

This perhaps naive hope was far from my reality. I was most often assumed White. If I was viewed as a person with albinism, again I was assumed White European. Most of my life I have had to prove my ethnicity. I have felt invisible. I reminded myself to step back and regard the situation more objectively. I understood that many people I met had no idea albinism occurred outside of Africa. I was evolving toward accepting this theory when another attendee mentioned casually that I didn't have African or Black features. I stared blank faced at her because I didn't even know how to respond to that statement.

In my twenties, I believed if I were in a crowd of hundreds of people with albinism or PWA I'd blend in. In reality, this has never happened. So why I thought I would have a different experience at the conference is unclear. It goes back to hope and longing. Part of me needed to be acknowledged and affirmed as a Black woman. And yet the only time this recognition occurred was when I pulled up a family photo on my phone to prove belonging. I had the anonymity I'd once pined for. Now, I didn't want it.

Intellectually I am well aware that how I choose to define myself holds the most importance. That if I identify as a Black woman, as a white-skinned Black woman, as a woman with albinism, that this is enough. However, my heart and my intellect duel with one another. And the child in me watches on the sidelines, awaiting an answer.

Sixty hours have passed, and I have slept, eaten, and released my hair. I contemplate my reflection, much in the way I did as a child. Freshly washed hair reminds me of soft, fluffy cotton candy beneath my fingertips. Veins are easily seen through the translucent skin of my hands. My face holds laugh lines on mostly smooth alabaster skin, and my lips are a soft pale pink, clearly defined. My eyes . . . well, they either appear red, pink, or blue, depending on the light. This is the me, completely unadorned, that I love.

COMING FULL CIRCLE

I believe my life patterns that of a spiral. On that circular path, I encounter and re-encounter issues of my life. The idea of belonging, of seeking to be part of a community, has always challenged me. And this quest to fit in, to sit comfortably within my skin, I can finally say I have conquered. This is not to dismiss the power of those moments or situations where I question myself, or recognize I am having "one of those days" of feeling other.

Once upon a time being part of the circle never entered my mind. I was too other, too different in appearance, too damaged. Just altogether too much. Yet during that time I lurked. I observed, I longed. Hell, I pined to play outdoors, to have friends, to resemble my brothers and sister, to be asked to school dances. I was a quiet, timid girl, frequently afraid of my own shadow. I possessed neither the code nor the currency of admittance. Yet I observed all the nuances of those who seemingly navigated with ease in these groups.

By the time I reached high school, I was part of a small, tight-knit group of kids. We were friends. We had classes together. Friday afternoons would find us boarding the N bus from Oakland to San Francisco. We were four, sometimes five, mostly studious, mostly sheltered, almost all gay and equally curious kids. Polk Street was the gay destination pre Castro Street. We would walk past sex shops and bars, eyes wide, taking in everything. Then we were off to the Coronet Theater or the Alexandria for a movie. Wanda, Anthony, Claire, and Danial were my posse. They were my first true experience of being part of something. And I loved it.

There came a time in my twenties when I, despite my fear, pushed myself, demanding insertion into the lesbian of color circle. We met in women's bookstores. We met in women's homes. We met at the Women's Building. Many times, I bore the brunt of hostility because of the color of my skin. This was a painful time for me. I desperately wanted to be part of the LOC, especially the Black lesbian community. I naively believed I would be welcomed because hey, I too am Black. But no. I encountered the same sense of being too other.

I found greater acceptance amongst the White lesbian literary community. My identity wasn't questioned. I simply was. Invisible.

I distinctly recall the defining moment of inserting myself into the circle to speak. I attended an event for Black lesbian writers at the now closed A Woman's Place Bookstore on Broadway. I went with a friend. It was a summer evening when we walked into the well-lit bookshop. There were so many women there. Immediately I wanted to flee. Even with a few years of therapy under my belt, anxiety and fear paralyzed me. The "Am I good enough? Am I Black enough?" and the pounding of my heart made my body hum. I turned to leave. Thankfully, my friend, also a very quiet woman who equally felt on the outside of the circle of Black sisterhood, steered me toward a seat, in an actual circle of course. We were all writers, all Black, all lesbian. And I am certain I was not the only one who was uncomfortable in that room. However, I was the only individual challenged for my right to be there.

We were given a writing prompt, which I no longer recall. One woman read hers, which attacked me directly for being a white-skinned woman in Black women's space. I felt my face redden, first in embarrassment, and second in anger. I was embarrassed because the voices in my head were loud. "I told you so. You don't belong here. You. Should. Just. Leave."

I looked for an exit. I started to rise, then I felt the calming hand of my friend on my arm. She whispered, "No, we are staying. Breathe." I took deep breaths to calm my heart. After a few minutes, I looked around the circle. I saw eyes that said, stay. Gazes that reassured me that I belonged. I began to write.

I wrote in response to the verbal attack. I wrote about my life having been a war of color. I shared my struggle to be accepted by Black women, Black lesbians.

Color Wars

My life has been a war of color, determining where I fit, where I belong. I am neither the coveted sweetest fruit of darkened berry nor the highest of yellow.

I feel rather than see your scorn directed like daggers at me. The unasked question of why I have come? Of why do I believe I have the right to be amongst you?

Always I must muster courage and surround myself with protective armor when attending these events because I know I am not welcomed. You see me as White though like you I too bear African blood. My ancestors were stolen from their villages, brought to this country in chains. Still all you see is the color of my skin.

Afterward the silence was profound. Eventually, the facilitator helped the group to move forward. For me the courage I'd had was momentous. It was the ultimate in me standing up for myself. For me, it was a beginning.

Years went by. I took my place as a parent, as part of a couple, as a woman who knew herself, who celebrated herself, and ultimately who no longer required the permission or the acceptance of others. I had taken my place within the circle with certainty.

Now with the passing of additional time I have come to recognize that I have stepped into the center of the circle. Surrounded with those who support and love me to do the work I must, to stand solidly in the now, I embrace the woman I have become. I am proud of my Blackness. I am proud of my albinism.

I used to want to be like someone else when I grew up. Now I have grown up, and I get to be me. Telling all the parts of myself that they get to grow up and be me, phenomenal, luscious, amazing me leaves me in the most beautiful iridescent puddle of tears.I am the newly born baby, the embodiment of truth. I am wonder and innocence shining brightly in a sea of prayer-fueled shame. I am the young girl whisked away to imaginary places within books when the sun restricts my movements. I am the teenager forced to conform for someone else's comfort, who in turn discovered otherness afforded me options. I am the young woman with newfound resilience amongst the sharp stones of ignorance. I am the seasoned woman, secure in my being, choosing to walk in grace.

The End

ACKNOWLEDGEMENTS

I am who I am in part to the many people who loved me, mentored me, advocated on my behalf and who stood by me when I could not do these things for myself. My mother, Annie Mary Young, instilled a love of literature which brings me joy daily. My mom, Carol Dean, who has believed in me from the beginning, who gently and sometimes not, brought me back to the work of writing. To my family, given and chosen, who recognized and honored the many times I opted out of events because of deadlines. I am grateful for my fiancée. Her continued love as well as providing reminders for sustenance and sleep help to keep me well.

Thank you to the To Live and Write in Alameda writing community. Most notably, Dafina, Jenee and Romny who read earlier versions of the book. Whose critiques enabled me to delve deeper in order to convey my story.

The support of my writing coach Dorothy Randall Gray and steadfast encouragement, belief in this project propelled me forward time and time again.

Special acknowledgement to Miriam Smolover, for accompanying me on my journey of healing.

Most importantly, my heart swells with love and gratitude for my daughter Jewel Devorawood as she inspires me live life fully.